RUNNING A BIG SHIP

The Big Ship

Running a Big Ship
The Classic Guide to Managing a Second World War Battleship

BY
Captain RORY O'CONOR, R.N.

Commander of HMS *Hood*, 1933–36

FOREWORD BY
Admiral THE EARL OF CORK AND ORRERY,
G.C.B., G.C.V.O.

Commander-in-Chief, Home Fleet,
1933–35

NEW INTRODUCTION BY
BRIAN LAVERY

CASEMATE

Oxford & Philadelphia

Published in Great Britain in 2017 by
CASEMATE PUBLISHERS
The Old Music Hall, 106–108 Cowley Road, Oxford OX4 1JE, UK

Originally published under the title *Running a Big Ship On 'Ten Commandments'*
(With Modern Executive Ideas and A Complete Organisation) (Portsmouth:
Gieves Ltd, 1937)

© Casemate Publishers 2017
Introduction © Brian Lavery 2017

Hardback Edition: ISBN 978-1-91086-019-9
Digital Edition: ISBN 978-1-61200-573-7 (epub)

A CIP record for this book is available from the British Library

Printed in the Czech Republic by FINIDR, s.r.o.
Typeset in India by Lapiz Digital Services, Chennai

For a complete list of Casemate titles, please contact:

CASEMATE PUBLISHERS (UK)
Telephone (01865) 241249
Fax (01865) 794449
Email: casemate-uk@casematepublishers.co.uk
www.casematepublishers.co.uk

INTRODUCTION

by Brian Lavery

Rory O'Conor, the author of *Running a Big Ship* (1937), was the son of a distinguished Irish surgeon. He entered the Naval College at Osborne on the Isle of Wight in September 1911 at the age of 13, and went on to Dartmouth three years later. He had first-class marks in seamanship, navigation and gunnery, but only a second in torpedo (which included a good deal of electrical work) and somehow missed out on engineering, perhaps because he, like all his colleagues, was rapidly promoted to midshipman on the outbreak of war in 1914 and sent to the fleet. O'Conor served three years in the old pre-Dreadnought battleship *Prince of Wales*, including the Dardanelles campaign. At first, he was only regarded as average, but soon began to attract attention as 'likely to make a good, steady and reliable officer'. He was commissioned as sub-lieutenant in 1917, and in the destroyers *Vivid* and *Walpole* he was regarded as 'exceptional'. After the war, there was some attempt to make up for O'Conor's lack of engineering knowledge when he was posted to the great battleship *Barham* for work in the engine room, then to the royal yacht *Victoria and Albert* for the same purpose. But when it was time for him to apply for a specialisation, it was made clear that he was not a candidate for the engineering branch, which would soon be separated from the seamen branch and greatly reduced in status. Instead, he went to HMS *Excellent*, the shore-based gunnery school at Portsmouth, to join the branch which regarded itself as the elite of the Royal Navy. By this time his references were invariably glowing, for example by Captain Dalglish in 1921:

> I have the highest opinion of this officer. Exceedingly capable and efficient; has an exceptionally good command of men; strict disciplinarian and a marked success as a divisional officer. Energetic, keen, hardworking and good organiser.[1]

O'Conor was a keen sportsman and remained a bachelor, which meant that his work for the navy was undistracted. He went on to serve as the gunnery officer of the *Resolution*, *Emerald* and *Royal*

---

[1] National Archives, ADM 196/146/696, 196/121/120, 196/93/26.

Sovereign, with time on the staff of *Excellent*, until the end of 1931 when he was promoted to commander and offered one of the best appointments in the Royal Navy.

HMS *Hood* was the star ship of the fleet, one of only three capital ships completed since the end of World War I. The battleships *Rodney* and *Nelson* were more powerful with their 16-inch guns and had much better armour protection, but they were modified during design to meet the restrictions of the Washington Treaty of 1922 and were known to the lower deck as 'the pair of boots' or 'the ugly sisters.' *Hood*, in contrast, was described by Derek Rayner of the Royal Naval Volunteer Reserve as 'the most beautiful steamship that man ever devised'.[2] She was seen around the world during the Special Service Cruise of 1923–4 when she took the future kings Edward VIII and George VI on a tour of the empire. The Coombs brothers, both boy seamen, were drafted to her in 1935 and thought it was a great honour.[3]

The commander of a battleship or cruiser was in fact the second-in-command of the ship, the head of the executive or seamen branch. As the chief organiser and motivator of the crew, he was far closer to the men than the captain, who was a remote figure. But O'Conor only had a general responsibility for the non-seaman branches such as engineering and the Royal Marines, which is reflected in the text of *Running a Big Ship* where they are hardly mentioned. An unspoken factor was the shadow of the Invergordon Mutiny of 1931. *Hood* had not been one of the leading ships when the men of the Atlantic Fleet refused to raise anchor, but her crew had followed the example of the *Rodney*, *Nelson* and *Valiant*. The mutiny was mainly about pay cuts which were to a certain extent rectified, but the effect on officers of losing their almost divine authority was traumatic. Moreover, it was recognised that the bad management and arrogance of some officers was a factor. Admiral Sir John Kelly described a 'failure to attend to the wants and grievances of the men,' and 'rowdy parties in officers' messes,' which would have led to disciplinary action if repeated on the lower deck. Such behaviour, according to Kelly, would never earn the praise, 'He's a proper gent, he is'.[4]

---

[2] D. A. Rayner, *Escort*, London, 1955, p 21.

[3] Imperial War Museum documents, 91/7/1.

[4] Brian Lavery, *Able Seamen,* London, 2011, p 295.

In fact, the *Hood* had been quite well run under Commander McCrum, but O'Conor began to apply a liberal regime, sympathetic to the men. He had some support from Admiral Sir William James who used the *Hood* as his flagship and had himself written *New Battleship Organisations* about the battle cruiser *Queen Mary* before the First World War.[5] O'Conor laid great stress on knowing the men's names, which became an article of faith among naval officers.[6] His 'Ten Commandments', like their biblical originals, were only a general basis for discipline, and were augmented by a great body of law and regulation. The commandments were based on consideration for others, good planning and, above all, timekeeping. According to O'Conor the commander should be fully involved, keeping his office door open and personally supervising the cleaning of the decks each morning.[7] The men were to be allowed all practicable liberties, and their messes were not to be changed except on the greatest necessity.[8] His notes on the organisation of the ship's air arm had only relevance for a limited period, but are revealing about this period in naval aviation.[9] He saw the need for a more practical seaman's uniform, which eventually arrived after World War II.[10] He dealt with the long-standing problem with midshipmen and suggested treating them as young officers rather than schoolboys.[11] A confirmed big-ship man, he only dealt with smaller ships such as destroyers by describing how the big ships could help them.[12] He has a good deal to say about sport and especially inter-ship regattas, in which *Hood*'s men excelled. He embraced the new inventions, sound films and wireless.[13] He says almost nothing about fighting, which was noticed by the critic of the *Naval Review*: 'It is, of course, implied that that a ship that is good at all these other things will by definition put up a good show in battle. This may well be so,

---

[5] Reprinted as *The Royal Naval Officer's Jutland Pocket Manual,* London, 2016.

[6] *Running a Big Ship,* pp 86–7.

[7] Ibid, pp 21–3, 47.

[8] Ibid, p 65.

[9] Ibid, pp 69–75.

[10] Ibid, p 99.

[11] Ibid, p 28.

[12] Ibid, pp 116–8.

[13] Ibid, pp 151–2.

but surely equal attention should be given to both aspects of the matter?'[14]

O'Conor left the *Hood* in 1936 and was keen to publicise his views on how ships should be run. He was given six months' paid leave to write the book, which he did in a study bedroom in his family home on the Isle of Wight, with the other occupants warned not to disturb him except in an emergency.[15] The book was published the following year. But not everyone accepted that his regime in the *Hood* had been successful. Captain Pridham claimed that she was 'the dirtiest ship I had ever seen' when he took over, and infested with cockroaches. He wrote that O'Conor was 'a first-class showman' but was 'obsessed with the idea of spoiling his ship's company by saving them trouble (i.e. work) and he rarely awarded any punishment.'[16] Louis le Bailly believed that O'Conor had treated the members of the sports teams more leniently, but later he adopted the Ten Commandments as engineer officer in the new battleship *Duke of York* in 1945.[17]

O'Conor and Pridham had very different philosophies, but the notes for newly joined officers compiled by Pridham in 1938 turned out to be more influential in the short term. Pridham was dealing with a different situation, of rapid expansion and in particular a shortage of experienced petty officers. His 'Notes' became the basis for a document issued to the hundreds of trainee wartime officers in HMS *King Alfred* in 1943, and are still regarded as 'Timeless wisdom in leadership'.[18] In contrast, O'Conor's book is restricted by its very title, for big ships became less important during World War II, which was dominated by destroyers, escort vessels, minesweepers, landing craft and coastal craft. O'Conor's dictum that 'the routine must go forward like clockwork'[19] was less relevant when all hands were under terrible stress and attack by aircraft or submarine might arrive at any moment. The number of capital ships did not increase, the arrival of the new ships of the *King George V* class was precisely matched by the loss of five

---

[14] *Naval Review,* May 1937, p 392.

[15] Nixie, Taverner, *A Torch Among the Tapers*, Bramber, 2000, p 255.

[16] Bruce Taylor, *The Battlecruiser HMS* Hood, Barnsley, 2004, pp 169–70.

[17] Louis le Bailly, *The Man around the Engine,* Emsworth, 1990, p 115.

[18] Published in *The Royal Navy Officer's Pocket Book,* ed. Lavery, London, 2006.

[19] *Running a Big Ship,* p 55.

others, including 'the mighty *Hood*' herself. Aircraft carriers had little to do with O'Conor's seamen-centred ideas – in 1939 the captain of the new *Ark Royal* pointed out that including aircrew he had more officers than able seamen and the messdecks were dominated by the technicians of the servicing crews.[20] Cruisers did however expand in numbers and *Running a Big Ship* was more relevant there. On the whole, the book reflects the peacetime era preceding the great naval expansion that began in 1936. It was also more relevant to the post-war era, not in its references to big ships which became increasingly rare, but in its concern for welfare, the education of young officers, the need for more practical uniforms and many other matters.

O'Conor went on to become a staff officer on the Joint Planning Committee in 1938–40 and was described as 'a cheerful, willing and unusually able staff officer, with great powers of work. He has a wide grasp of strategical problems and inclines to orthodox views and the rejection of any ideas tainted with unsoundness.' In May 1940, he took command of the cruiser *Neptune*, where he was very effective but his lack of recent experience in ship handling proved a drawback – contrary to the tradition that the captain should direct the ship himself, he used his navigating officer to guide him during difficult manoeuvres.[21] He was lost when the *Neptune* struck a mine in the Mediterranean in December 1941. If he had lived, he would almost certainly have risen to high rank and his experience and ideas would have proved invaluable in the much-needed social reform of the post-war navy.

---

[20] *Transactions of the Institution of Naval Architects,* 1939, p 12.
[21] *A Torch Among the Tapers,* pp 282–3.

To

'…the revolutionary constitutionalist…'
Seven Pillars of Wisdom (1935), p 141

PREFACE

It is with some trepidation that a man should decide to put his own experience into print. Individual experience is bound to have severe limitations, and to presume to set up one's own as a beacon to others is to risk misleading the few who are likely to follow the light. But if it is regarded only as forming one more stepping-stone to a better state, then one feels encouraged to persevere, and to attempt the task of laying a modest stone in its place.

Experience at sea is as varied as in any other sphere, and many will hold widely divergent views from those expressed here. I am only giving opinions based on my own observation, and if sentences are not continually prefaced with 'I consider' or 'in my opinion,' it is in order to avoid tiresome repetition, and it does not mean that I am presuming to lay down the law.

I sought for expert assistance in dealing with two important new-comers to the executive fold—the Aircraft and the High-Speed Boat. The chapter on 'The Ship's Air Arm' is contributed by Lieutenant-Commander Douglas MacKendrick, R.N., whilst the section on 'Modern High-Speed Service Boats' is the work of Lieutenant-Commander Peter du Cane, R.N. (retired).

I am grateful for much assistance obtained from *New Battleship Organisations* (Commander W. M. James, 1915), and to *A Cruiser Commander's Orders* (Commander R. Grenfell, 1933).

The 'Executive Organisation' given in Part II was compiled prior to commissioning, and has now been completely revised on the experience of three years in commission. It has been arranged so as to be easily adaptable to ships of all sizes and classes.

I have tried to avoid making this into a book of 'don'ts,' in obedience to the modernist belief in the power of positive suggestion; in the same way, our 'Ten Commandments' have been kept free of the negation, 'Thou shalt not!'

R. O'C.

FOREWORD

IT was with great pleasure that I accepted the invitation of an old friend, the author of this book, to write a Foreword to his work. That pleasure was increased when I had the opportunity of reading the MS., for therein I found the explanation of the success obtained by the application of these orders. To that success I can testify, for *Hood* recommissioned for this particular commission within a few days of the date on which I hoisted my flag in command of the Fleet. She started with a swing and never looked back. At the end of my two years, *Hood* was an example to the Fleet in all the work and other activities with which this book deals.

Although the book may be primarily intended to help the Commander about to commission a large ship, it can be recommended to the study of all officers who wish to succeed in an 'executive capacity'—which means in the commanding and leading of men; for it is based upon those principles that must be applied if a success is to be made of this difficult task. The rules, directions, and advice given are all simple and clear. It is evident that they are framed with careful regard to the comfort and well-being of those whom they affect, and with a view to imposing no more restraint on the individual than is necessary to ensure the efficiency of the ship and the interests of all who serve in her.

Young and old alike are encouraged to consider themselves as in part responsible for the establishment and maintenance of the reputation of the ship. It is by these means that the best results are obtained. Every individual is stimulated to an effort if he can be made to feel that he counts, that he is of real value and can help, and is not merely one of a crowd. If each member of a community can be inspired in this way, it goes far to create a healthy public opinion and *esprit de corps,* the strongest deterrents against any misdeeds on the part of individuals.

By giving orders with the support of the Naval Discipline Act, you can to a great extent control a man's actions, but you cannot control his thoughts. These are governed by his ideas. It is only by suggesting the ideas you want to inculcate, that you will get him to think as you wish him to, and thereby obtain his full support.

And with the men with whom we are privileged to work that is not difficult, for the great majority start with the right ideas, and are anxious to follow a lead that coincides with their views. Nowadays there is only a small minority that need any coercion. The value of such public opinion was well shown during the visit of the Fleet to the Thames in the spring of 1935. During the week spent there, *Hood* had only one absentee—and he was held up by a traffic jam—in spite of the boundless hospitality of Southend and the near-by attractions of London: a triumph, even in these days, when the size of her ship's company, and the numerous changes always taking place, are taken into account.

Having achieved this, it was not surprising that *Hood* swept the board at the annual regatta a few weeks later—a result which is referred to with pardonable pride in the chapter devoted to the preparation for that event. The ship's company that can make a collective effort in one direction can usually make it in others. There are, of course, those who affect to sneer at such successes, saying that the Navy does not exist solely for boat-racing or other competitive drills and recreations. That may be partly true. But the Navy does exist to make great collective efforts under the most difficult conditions.

The ship whose officers and men, of all departments alike, are accustomed to go all out for the honour of their ship, is likely to last out just that fraction of a minute longer than an opponent, which in battle makes all the difference between victory and defeat. Those who 'pull harder than the rest' are likely to 'fight harder' also. In the building up of this spirit lies the real importance of the Executive Officer's duties. It is still true, in the words of the late Admiral Sir Reginald Custance, that:

> 'Battles are won or lost by men, not ships.'

But let no reader of this book conclude that the literal application of these orders and ideas is all that is necessary to obtain the desired results. It is also necessary for those who administer them to show an example of enthusiasm, zeal, and self-sacrifice. Only thus can the written word be translated into successful action.

In the words of St. Paul:

'THE LETTER KILLETH, BUT THE SPIRIT QUICKENETH.'

Cork & Orrery

Admiral.

CONTENTS

PART I

RUNNING A BIG SHIP

DISCIPLINE

CLEANLINESS

TRAINING

MISCELLANEOUS IDEAS

RECREATION

PART II

LIST OF ILLUSTRATIONS

PART I

I. The 'Ten Commandments'
and
Modern Executive Ideas

SHIP'S STANDING ORDERS

1. *The Service.*—The Customs of the Service are to be observed at all times.

2. *The Ship.*—The Good Appearance of the Ship is the concern of everyone in *Hood,* and all share the responsibility for this.

3. *The Individual.*—Every man is constantly required to bring credit to the Ship by his individual bearing, dress and general conduct, on board and ashore.

4. *Courtesy to Officers.*—The courtesy of making a gangway, and standing to one side to attention when an Officer passes, is to be shown by every man.

If an Officer passing through men during stand-easy, meal hours, etc., carries his cap under his arm, it will indicate that no attention, other than clearing a gangway, is required.

5. *Execution of Orders.*—All orders, including those passed by Bugle and Pipe, are to be obeyed at the Run.

6. *Punctual Attendance at Place of Duty.*—Every man is personally responsible, on all occasions, for his own punctual attendance at his place of duty.

7. *Permission to Leave Work.*—A man is always to ask permission before leaving his work.

8. *Reporting on Completion of Work.*—Any man on finishing the work for which he has been told off, is to report to his immediate superior. Parties of men are to be fallen in and reported.

9. *Card-playing and Gambling.*—While card-playing is allowed at mess tables and on the upper deck, any form of gambling is strictly prohibited. Gambling includes all games of chance played for money stakes.

10. *Requests.*—Any man wishing to see the Commander is to put in a request to his Officer of Division. In urgent cases his request is to pass through the M.A.A. and O.O.W.

'He wished to live a life of discipline and order in which all went well so long as a man did his duty, and in which he might be free from uncertainty as to what his duty was; in which he had to obey, and in which it was enough for him to be an honest and a gallant man.'

EUGÈNE DE BEAUHARNAIS.

'TEN COMMANDMENTS'

When you come to commission a ship your mind turns to the question of getting out the necessary orders.

In the first place, a simple and clearly worded code of laws seems to be required, which shall be applicable to every soul on board and always in his sight. If Moses could control the people of Israel for forty years in the desert with Ten Commandments, it would be surprising if more were needed for the commission of a ship. This code forms the Ship's Standing Orders, and it is the 'little' which everyone must know.

The function of the Standing Orders should be regarded as entirely separate from the Executive Organisation, which forms the second part of this book. In the former, a general standard of conduct is laid down, while the latter provides a guide and reference on the detailed running of the ship, for all those set in authority, and comprises a great deal which relatively few people need to know.

On page 3 are shown the Ship's Standing Orders which were found effective throughout a commission. A few words are needed to enlarge on these orders when explaining them to the ship's company.

1. *The Service.*—'*The Customs of the Service are to be observed at all times.*' It may be argued that this is redundant. That may be so, but every officer and man of every branch, on entering the Service, is carefully schooled in the Customs of the Service. These Customs mean much to us, and the plain statement that our ship is one in which they are observed can do no harm, and may be a helpful reminder.

2. *The Ship.*—'*The Good Appearance of the Ship is the concern of everyone on board, and all share the responsibility for this.*' It is sometimes lightly assumed that the ship's appearance is the concern only of a small hierarchy which includes the Commander, the Chief Boatswain's Mate, the Captains of the Tops and the Side, and perhaps a few others. No ship was ever kept clean except by the co-operation of all hands, and this needs hammering in, with emphasis on the ways in which every individual can help:

(*a*) No leaning on the paintwork.
(*b*) No leaning on the guardrails.
(*c*) No fag-ends, matches or other rubbish on the deck.
(*d*) No throwing slops out of scuttles.
(*e*) No one improperly dressed on deck.

Everyone must be jealous of the ship's appearance and must make his contribution, and above all, he must avoid making unnecessary work for others who are striving to keep the ship as she should look.

If a man is caught leaning on the paintwork, throwing fag-ends or any other rubbish on the deck, emptying slops out of a scuttle, leaning on the guardrails, or in fact doing anything which not only spoils the ship's appearance but, worse still, spoils some other man's good work, then put him as a sentry on the upper deck after hours, and leave him there until he catches someone else offending against the ship; that man then goes before the Officer of the Watch and takes over as a sentry. The operation of this system of sentries must be kept under the personal control of the O.O.W., to avoid risk of abuse. Setting a thief to catch a thief is the policy which works well, and has a sporting element about it.

In the early days of a commission you will get as many as forty paintwork sentries in the course of a single make-and-mend afternoon; but when the battle for the ship's appearance has been fought and won, there will be very few indeed.

3. *The Individual.*—*'Everyone is constantly required to bring credit to the ship by his individual bearing, dress and general conduct, on board and ashore.'* This embraces a multitude of small points which go to the making of a fine ship's company, and leads in turn to that which has been described as England's Best Ambassador— 'a British Blue-Jacket walking ashore in a foreign port.'

Being on deck in an improper rig is another offence against the ship's good appearance, for which the 'sentry' system is a suitable deterrent.

4. *Courtesy to Officers.*—*'The courtesy of making a gangway and standing to one side to attention when an Officer passes is to be shown by every man.*

'If an Officer passing through men during stand-easy, meal hours, etc., carries his cap under his arm, it will indicate that no attention, other than clearing a gangway, is required.' This needs careful explanation to the ship's company. No one wants to delay work—all that is required by the first part of this order is that the gangway shall be cleared by standing to one side to attention. Men working clear of the gangway should never be required to stop work and stand to attention because an officer is passing.

The second part of this order has proved most useful, and it might well be headed 'Consideration for the Men.' There are

'. . . England's Best Ambassadors . . .'

many occasions when an officer has to pass through men during stand-easy, or after working hours, and when going on the mess-deck during meal hours; the cap carried under the arm gives a clear and unmistakable indication that no attention other than clearing a gangway is required. It makes a definite contribution to the ideal state of every man knowing what is required of him, and facilitates officers in moving freely about the ship, after hours, without disturbing the men.

5. *Execution of Orders.*—'*All orders, including those passed by Bugle and Pipe, are to be obeyed at the Run.*' Naturally there are occasions, such as when carrying heavy weights and fragile stores, or in rough weather and in crowded gangways, when this is not possible, but it should be laid down as a guiding principle and insisted on from the start of the commission.

6. *Punctual Attendance at Place of Duty.*—'*Every man is personally responsible on all occasions for his own punctual attendance at his place of duty.*' This is a simple issue and gives the answer in advance to the old excuse, 'Didn't hear the pipe.' A straightforward and regular routine, ordered by bugle and pipe, and amended as necessary by the Commander's Daily Orders, leaves no excuse for any man not being at the right place and at the right time.

7. *Permission to Leave Work.*—'*Before leaving his work, a man is always to ask permission.*'

8. *Reporting on Completion of Work.*—'*Any man on finishing the work for which he has been told off, is to report to his immediate superior. Parties of men are to be fallen in and reported.*' Both (7) and (8) are intended for the skulker—the man who is prepared to slip away and leave the rest of his topmates to do the work. All the world hates a skulker—it must hate him—why should a man slide away and leave his mates to finish off a job, perhaps an unpleasant one and in bad weather? The worst of skulking is that it can easily become infectious—stop it at once. There is only one treatment for deliberate skulking, and that is '14 days No. 11.' Allow no cutting of corners on the routine—when you sound 'Cooks,' that means Cooks only to the galley. This needs much care and determination in the early days of a commission, and it must be impressed on everyone that you intend to have 'NO SKULKING.'

9. *Card-playing and Gambling.*—'*While card-playing is allowed at mess tables and on the upper deck, any form of gambling is strictly prohibited. Gambling includes all games of chance played for money stakes*' A King's Regulation which should be kept well to the fore.

10. *Requests.—'Any man wishing to see the Commander is to put in a request to his Officer of Division. In urgent cases his request is to pass through the M.A.A. and O.O.W.'* This is the last of the 'Commandments,' and it is of the first importance. In a great ship's company, there must inevitably arise every variety of problem for the individuals composing it—problems of life, love, leave, illness, death, and hardship of all kinds arising from work, pay, food, sleep, to mention only a few. No request must be ignored—all must be considered and given a sympathetic hearing, and the men encouraged to come forward.

Making the Standing Orders known.—Steps taken to do this include:

1. On first commissioning, the entire ship's company to be shown the orders on lantern slides, one order at a time, on a screen under the Quarterdeck awning, the company sitting on the deck, and each order being explained as above.

2. A framed copy of the Standing Orders on each Messdeck. A large copy to be framed and mounted in some recreation space or smoking place.

3. Every officer and rating joining after the commission has started, to have the orders fully explained to him by the Commander.

Enforcing the Standing Orders.—Making a reality of the 'Ten Commandments' is, of course, a responsibility that lies with everyone in a position of authority in the ship—there must be no laxity in enforcement. A weekly summary of offences against the orders should be published. Typical summaries at the beginning and end of a commission, respectively, are included at the end of this chapter.

If the Commander has a framed copy of the Standing Orders, always placed before him on his Defaulters' Table, he will find that he can without difficulty connect 99 per cent. of the offences directly to one of the 'Commandments.'

They must be kept alive!

H.M.S. *HOOD*

Offences against Ship's Standing Orders

Week ending . . . . 193.

(A typical summary in early days of the commission.)

2. THE SHIP:

Leaning on the paintwork . . .	Sentries — 1 A.B., 2 Ords., 1 Tel. and 18 Boys.
Leaning on the gunwale . . .	Sentries — 3 Stokers, 2 Ords. and 4 Boys.
Improperly dressed . . .	Sentries — 1 Sig., 1 Boy.
Smoking in an improper place . .	2 Signalmen.
Throwing matches on deck . .	Sentries — 1 A.B., 2 Mnes., 1 Ord., Tel.
Throwing cigarette ends on the deck	1 Mne., 1 Boy.

3. THE INDIVIDUAL:

Returning from leave drunk . .	1 Stoker.
Negligently stowing clothes in locker .	2 Boys.
Disrespectful to a Chief Petty Officer .	1 Cook.
Failed to sling a clean hammock .	1 Signalman.
Smoking during working hours .	1 Ord. Sig.

5. EXECUTION OF ORDERS:

Slack in falling in at Divisions . .	1 Ord.

6. PUNCTUAL ATTENDANCE AT PLACE OF DUTY:

Absent over leave	3 Stokers and 2 Ords.
Absent from Quarters Clean Guns .	8 Ords.
Absent from place of duty . .	1 A.B., 3 Ords. R.N.V.R.
Absent from Hands fall in . .	1 Ord.

7. PERMISSION TO LEAVE WORK:

Skulking from his place of duty .	1 Boy Tel.
Leaving the Forecastle without permission	1 A.B. (14 Days No. 11).

H.M.S. *HOOD*

Offences against Ship's Standing Orders

Week ending . . . . 193.

(A typical summary *later* in the commission.)

2. THE SHIP:

Throwing a cigarette end on the deck 1 Ord. (Sentry).

3. THE INDIVIDUAL:

Improperly dressed on shore . . . 1 Ord.
Drunk whilst on shore . . . . 1 Ord. Sig.

6. PUNCTUAL ATTENDANCE AT PLACE OF DUTY:

Absent over leave . . . . . 1 A.B., 1 Stoker, 1 Cook.
Absent from sea-boat . . . . 1 Ord.

EXECUTIVE OFFICERS

II. THE EXECUTIVE TEAM

The Commander is at the head of a department, which in a big ship includes some forty Commissioned, Subordinate and Warrant Officers.

If they are to work as a team, it is necessary that they should know what is going on, and that they should be generally well informed as to executive policy and requirements. For this reason, a weekly meeting of the Executive Officers serves the good purpose of keeping the whole team working together as one. It may be found more convenient to see the Midshipmen separately, but it should be easy enough to find time for both meetings each week.

The Commander must keep a note of all points cropping up during the week, and he should have his agenda clearly prepared before the meetings. Likely matters for inclusion are:

Expressed wishes of the Captain.

Next week's programme, including (G.), (T.) and Air and Working Party requirements.

Officers' duties.

Mistakes on watch.

The boats.

Disciplinary matters.

Defaulters and requests—points arising from.

Leave and libertymen.

Appearance of the ship—faults found.

Uniform.

Training and advancement.

Sport, recreation and health.

Important signals and future movements of the ship.

These are only a few of the myriad points which arise in the course of a commission, affecting some or all of the Executive Team.

It is far simpler, quicker, and more efficient to have a weekly meeting than to be circulating endless notices to officers, or, alternatively, to be pointing out the same mistake to every officer in turn. The meetings encourage a spirit of co-operation, and lead to a free exchange of ideas; many interesting suggestions are put forward, making for the steady and progressive development of executive policy in the ship.

Another valuable service performed by this Executive Officers Committee is in the collective consideration of the half-yearly recommendations for advancement. The character and ability of a rating may come within the knowledge of others besides his Divisional Officer, and in regard to these recommendations there is no better means of arriving at an answer which will carry confidence than in discussion by a group of officers, who have acquired from regular practice the habit of sharing and exchanging opinions round a table.

There is no need for the meetings to be long-drawn-out affairs: twenty minutes to half an hour is usually quite enough. They are of special value in the early months of the commission, and it is well worth carrying them on right through, in order to maintain a strong executive team spirit. It is not always easy for subordinates to speak their true minds, especially when their views seem opposed to those held by the Commander. It is essential, however, that he should hear them, and the weekly meetings help to keep him readily and regularly accessible to the ideas of others.

> 'When a man opposes me, he should awake my attention, not my anger. . . . The cause of truth should be the common cause of both of us.'—MONTAIGNE.

III.   SHARING THE EXECUTIVE WORK

1. *Officer of the Watch.*—The King's Regulations which determine the responsibilities and authority of the Officer of the Watch deserve special attention, if only to remind us of the weight of responsibility for the safety of the ship which he shoulders, and of his authoritative position, with everyone on board subordinated to him but the Captain, the Executive Officer, and, in the Captain's absence, the Commanding Officer for the time being.

In fact, the duty of Officer of the Watch in a big ship is too important and onerous to be treated as the concern of only the more junior officers.

The Junior Lieutenant, in common with every other commissioned officer in the Executive Team, has his ship and action duties to attend to—probably a Division and a Turret—and it is therefore only fair that 'Officer of the Watch,' in harbour and at sea, should be shared by the whole team as part of the executive work. If everyone from the First Lieutenant to the Junior Warrant Officer does his turn no one is overburdened, and 'Officer of the Watch' is very properly enhanced in prestige. Otherwise it becomes the monotonous preoccupation of a few junior officers, to the exclusion of their other duties.

2. *Commanding Officer.*—The Commanding Officer is at all times the Senior Executive Officer on board—he is the man who takes charge and gives decisions in emergency and who, when necessary, must shoulder the responsibility of command.

The expression 'Duty C.O.,' which is sometimes heard, is wrong, as it confuses functions. The Duty Lieutenant-Commander may happen to be the Senior Executive Officer on board, and in that case he is also Commanding Officer for the time being; but the position of 'Commanding Officer' is a question of seniority and not of turn of duty.

3. *Duty Officers,* (a) *Duty Lieutenant-Commander.*—He takes over the Executive Officer's routine duties when ordered to do so after working hours, and he should then carry a telescope to indicate his duty to all concerned. He may be called on at any time to act for the Commander.

Turn of duty . . . . . 24 hours.
Commences duty . . . . 0900.
Goes Lower Rounds at . . . 2100.
Keeps Middle Watch in harbour.
When he is the Senior Executive Officer on board he is also
 Commanding Officer.

(*b*) *Stand-by Officer.*—Only if there are sufficient officers to admit of a middle group. He is a Senior Lieutenant.

He may be called on to take charge of any big work which is going on.

He can be called on to assist the O.O.W. if pressure of work on the upper deck is excessive.

When Officer of the Watch is below the rank of Lieutenant, the Stand-by Officer is called on to deal with defaulters (*vide* 'Captain's Standing Orders').

He takes Patrols, and Officer of the Guard.

Turn of duty . . . . . . 24 hours.
Commences duty . . . . . 0900.
Keeps Morning Watch in harbour.

The Stand-by Officer is not intended to fulfil the somewhat dubious and uncertain function of Officer of the Day, found in some big ships. The latter tends to become nothing but an additional botherer of the Officer of the Watch, although he has no authority to do so under King's Regulations. The Stand-by Officer, in common with all other officers, excepting only three, is subordinate to the Officer of the Watch when the latter is in the performance of his duties.

(*c*) *Duty Lieutenants.*—These include all other Lieutenants and Sub-Lieutenants, R.N., R.M., and R.N.R.

They keep Watch from 0830 to 2400 in harbour.
Two officers are always to be on board.
Turn of duty . . . . . . 24 hours.

(*d*) *Warrant Officer of the Day.*—His special duties are laid down in the Executive Organisation. He is available to assist the O.O.W. at any time on the upper deck.

Turn of duty . . . . . . 24 hours.
Commences duty . . . . . 0730.
Relieves the deck as O.O.W. from 0730 to 0830 in
 harbour.
Second Officer of the Watch at sea as required.

4. *Confusion of Duties.*—The confusion and duplication of the duties and functions of the executive team are among the

chief reasons which make the Officer of the Watch in a big ship sometimes feel that his life is a burden to him.

The regulations require that he shall serve only three masters, and not more than two of these at one time. The executive work must be shared and arranged so as to ensure that these conditions always obtain. The two masters should speak with a single voice, soft pedal down, and only when necessary.

5. *Mate of the Upper Deck.*—With regard to the duty of Mate of the Upper Deck, the issue has frequently been raised that the horizontal control of the upper deck, implied by having an officer to act in this capacity under the Commander, conflicts with the vertical sovereignty of the Officers of Divisions. In actual fact there is no need for any such conflict to arise, as the chief function of the Mate of the Upper Deck, in relation to the parts of ship, is that of a co-ordinator and an adviser, and not an administrator.

If the right man, and a tactful one, is available for this duty, he can play an important part in the work and organisation of the upper deck, especially if he has had previous experience as executive officer of smaller ships. The Commander who is able to enlist the services of an experienced destroyer officer as his mate is indeed fortunate, and his load is lightened thereby.

The duties of the Mate of the Upper Deck, preferably a Lieutenant-Commander, may be summarised as follows:

(*a*) *Upper Deck.*—He understudies the Commander, and, where necessary, co-ordinates the work of the seamen divisions on the upper deck, and for outside painting and cleanliness.

(*b*) *Boat Officer.*—He acts as Boat Officer, being responsible for the upkeep and repair of a flotilla of some twenty boats; he takes the boat stores on charge.

He produces the boat routines, and provides the necessary boats to enable the Officer of the Watch to maintain the required services.

He supervises the selection and training of coxswains.

(*c*) *Boys' Division.*—The Boys' Division fits in well with his other work, as he then has a particular interest in, and knowledge of, untrained personnel working in all the seamen parts of ship.

(*d*) *Central Stores.*—He maintains a close liaison with the Central Storekeeping Officer, and generally regulates the issue of stores and of cleaning gear to the parts of ship; collecting the necessary oars for the regatta is another of his duties, which requires much contrivance.

(*e*) *General.*—He associates himself with the work of the Boatswain, of the Sailmaker and of the Captain of the Side, and keeps the Commander informed of their requirements.

The fact of the Mate of the Upper Deck fulfilling these wide functions does not mean that the Commander himself becomes an inaccessible Olympian, out of touch with officers and petty officers.

The Commander cannot always be sure of being able to give immediate attention to any one section of his executive work, and decentralisation is therefore as necessary on the upper deck as elsewhere, if the work is to go steadily forward.

The Commander and his Mate must keep in close touch, or there will be a danger of conflicting policies and orders.

IV.   THE COMMANDER'S ACCESSIBILITY

In the course of the day's work innumerable people have business to do with the Commander of a big ship, and his ready accessibility is a matter of importance. Even with a properly decentralised organisation, it is inevitable that the Commander should be constantly sought after for consultation, advice, approval, permission, information, and a hundred and one other reasons. In addition, he must be at hand, especially in flagships, to receive visiting senior officers at the gangway.

Inaccessible versus *Accessible.*—An inaccessible man may be defined as one who

    (*a*) can never be found, or
    (*b*) invariably expresses annoyance at being interrupted.

People soon cease to seek out a man like these, with a result that he loses touch, and so much the worse for the ship.

The Commander wants to feel free to wander about the ship at will, seeing the hands at work and getting to know them. But there is a time for everything, and there should be at least one hour, both in the forenoon and afternoon, when the whole ship knows that there is *one* place where he can almost certainly be found, and available.

Outward and Visible Signs.—His cabin is probably the best position in which he can come to rest, and once he is fixed, there are certain outward and visible signs of accessibility to be attended to:

    (*a*) Cabin door open and curtain drawn back.
    (*b*) Sitting at a table facing the door.
    (*c*) Never too preoccupied to glance up at once and greet the caller with 'Come in.'
    (*d*) A chair ready placed for the caller to sit on.

The very reverse of accessible is the man who sits writing with his back to a closed door, fails to notice you on first arrival, then looks up, and with irritation or impatience says 'What do you want?'

The Commander of a ship needs separate day and sleeping cabins, as it is disconcerting, when transacting official business, for him to be constantly interrupted by the necessary coming and going of his servant, and it is hard on the latter to be turned out in the middle of his work.

A Suggested Technique.—The late Lord Inchcape had a technique in dealing with subordinates reporting difficulties or problems:

1. *Listen.*
2. *Question* until understood.
3. *Ask* for a remedy.
4. *Weigh* it.
5. *Decide:* Yes or No.
6. If *No,* give reasons if time permits.

In a matter of urgency it may be necessary for a superior to give an immediate decision without awaiting a subordinate's proposals, but, normally, the latter is only half doing his work if, when he comes along with a problem, he fails to suggest a solution. The Commander must take care not to develop into a penny-in-the-slot machine, into which others drop their difficulties and expect the answer to fall out.

This is one of the worst forms of centralisation.

Off Duty.—Like everyone else, the Commander feels the need of leisure time, and after hours he may well turn his executive duties over to the Duty Lieutenant-Commander. Having done so, he is entitled to shut his door and settle down to a book, with orders not to call him when it comes on to blow, but when it has stopped blowing.

If Punctuality is the first virtue in the Commander of a ship, then Accessibility assuredly comes second.

'. . . Signs of Accessibility . . .'

V. THE COMMANDER AND THE SPECIALISTS

Head of Department.—The Commander of a ship is the head of the Executive Department, in which those ship's officers who are specialists have an important function.

The specialists, whether Air, Gunnery, Navigation, Signals or Torpedo, are *not* heads of departments.

They are, of course, the Captain's direct and personal advisers in respect of their weapons and of their particular technical knowledge. But in all matters of internal organisation, administration and discipline, their work falls within the Executive Department, and the responsibility of co-ordination devolves on the Commander.

A Specialist Officer's Duties:

First: an Executive Officer and a Seaman.
Secondly: a Technical Specialist.

Specialisation is nothing very much by itself, but it is the fillip which helps the *good* Executive Officer to go ahead in the Service.

He must not be cold-shouldered into thinking he is mainly a specialist. Nearly everyone tries to help him to make this mistake—look at our self-evident nickname habit: 'Guns,' 'Torps,' 'Flags,' and now even 'Ping'! It is as well not to initiate or prolong discussion of one's own brand of technical 'shop' in the Wardroom.

Executive Openings for Specialists.—It is up to the specialist to seize his executive openings, and here are some of the possibilities:

(1) Cable Officer (First, Second or even Third).
(2) Officer of the Watch at sea.
(3) Officer of Division.
(4) In charge of a messdeck.
(5) To run at least one game and to support all.
(6) A part of watch, a boat or a derrick at General Drill.
(7) Main Derrick.
(8) Snotties' Nurse.
(9) Sailing races.
(10) *Divisions and Quarters*—always attend if on board.
(11) When you are Duty Lieutenant-Commander or Officer of the Day, run the Executive Department after working hours, on the Commander's behalf.

And there are many more openings for the specialists, who cannot do too much general executive work when little may be expected of them.

Specialist Co-operation with the Commander.

(*a*) *Stations.*—The Watch Bill being based on the Quarter Bill, be considerate for the Commander's wants and wishes.

(*b*) *Drills.*—Think well ahead. Ask only for what is needed, and ask in plenty of time. The Commander has to make out his programme the previous afternoon, and therefore the specialists' needs must be decided in the forenoon.

(*c*) *Ship's Appearance.*—Be sure that the weapons never let down the ship's appearance.

(*d*) *Information.*—Keep the Commander very fully informed of all that is intended and that is being planned for the future, and bring all the information possible to the weekly meetings of the Executive Officers.

VI.   MIDSHIPMEN

Midshipmen are seen differently by different people:

By the thoughtless . . as messengers.

By the Training and Educa-
tional experts (whose name
is legion, for they are
many) } as schoolboys and their natural prey.

And, lastly, by those who
regard them { as officers and beings like our selves, and who, as they are younger, have not yet had time to make all our mistakes.

A Midshipman is an officer, and must be treated as such and given a task which he feels he can make his own, whether in charge of a boat or as Midshipman of the Watch, and only his Action Station must take precedence. Once he realises that he will be treated with the full consideration due to his status as an officer, no one gives a readier response than a Midshipman, in keenness on his job and on the ship, both in her work and in her play.

If an officer is constantly called away in the middle of doing his proper executive work to attend instruction, one day when he goes back he will find he is no longer wanted—the Cox-swain will have usurped charge of the boat, and the Quarter-master charge of the watch—and the Midshipman will feel that he is of no use to anyone.

Midshipmen of Boats.—The finest training as a seaman and for command that he can possibly have is in a boat if he is given complete charge. Should the boat have two crews, there should be a Midshipman for each, working only with his own crew, and hoisted in and out with them in the boat.

The Commander should require a personal report from the Midshipman on any mishap to his boat, and he should be satisfied if it is clear that the lesson has been learnt. Mistakes have their uses, and a picket boat smashed may one day mean a battleship saved. The traditional leave-stopping seems a pointless and humiliating procedure.

The Midshipman of a boat must share all vicissitudes of wind and weather with his crew, and it is not right for him to accept an invitation to go below in another ship while his boat lies off, with the crew exposed to the elements.

He should, however, man and leave his boat at the gangway and not over the lower boom, and it is part of his duty to see that she is properly made fast, or moored up, before he goes below.

Midshipman of the Watch.—He is not a messenger.

He is Second Officer of the Watch, and should have complete charge of routine and take over the deck in the O.O.W.'s absence.

Running the routine is an important task and can be made interesting. If it runs like clockwork the effect on the ship is magical.

There is no limit to the help that an efficient Midshipman of the Watch can give to the Commander.

Midshipmen's Leave Book.—The Leave Book should be abolished. If it is decided to treat them as officers, the question of leave is covered by the Captain's Standing Orders: 'Officers are free to go ashore, out of working hours, when clear of duty.'

The head of the Executive Department must dislike seeing one of his subordinates compelled to thread his way through a crowd of officers in the ante-room in order to solicit the signature of, say, an instructor officer (and no disrespect is meant) so that Midshipmen may have permission to go ashore.

The leave of officers in the Executive or any other department is a matter between them as individuals and their Captain, through the head of their department. The Leave Book is an outworn survival of the 'schoolboy' attitude to Midshipmen.

Naturally, the time at which their leave expires depends on a variety of circumstances, and it only requires an order laying down what is decided. But it is as well to remember, before restricting their leave, that young men of their age, 18 to 20, of all branches on the lower deck, can have leave normally to 2200 on any night of the year, and this is now usually extended to 2300 for the cinema.

Schoolboy Punishments.—Punishments that are suitable for schoolboys are not suitable for adolescents of the ages of 18 to 21 whom it is intended to regard as officers. We must have it one way or the other. Either treat them as schoolboys—messengers, truants—or else make up our minds that they are officers and that we are going to treat them as such.

The old argument, that a Snottie preferred half a dozen to having his leave stopped, is disposed of when it is realised that neither treatment is suitable for an officer.

'. . . Compulsion breeds Dislike . . .'

It is rare to find an officer who, having had a fault corrected, does not make up his mind it shall not happen again. The rare exceptions are by no means confined to Midshipmen.

Naval Instruction Needs.—A certain number of hours' instruction a week must be done. Careful organisation can provide for this without violating the principle that the Midshipman's boat or his watch comes first. If a boat is run by two crews, her Midshipmen must be detailed from different sections. Similarly the watch-keepers are not all provided by one section. Dovetailing of duties is required.

Early Morning Physical Jerks.—Compulsion breeds dislike! Everyone knows that regular physical exercise as a means to a certain desirable end is good for us. But proof is needed that anything but a depression of the spirit comes from compulsory physical jerks for a group of officers on a wet and slippery deck before breakfast. And as a diverting exhibition for stray ordinary seamen and others scrubbing decks, it serves neither the cause of discipline nor the cause of cleanliness.

A Midshipman leads an active life in charge of his boat or on watch, and when added to that he plays games, and walks or runs whenever he can, compulsory physical drill before breakfast is nothing less than an infliction, which is likely to fill him with a lasting dislike.

Physical exercises are a valuable help to fitness at sea, when done of the free will and at the right time of day.

The Commander and the Midshipmen.—The Midshipmen are among the Commander's right-hand men. They run the boats and they run his routine for him—it is only right that they should know what he wants and what is going on.

If the Commander has a weekly meeting of the Midshipmen, it provides the opportunity to discuss all the week's happenings on the upper deck: in the boats, disciplinary matters, explaining where mistakes occurred and raising a host of miscellaneous points, past, present and future, connected with themselves, the ship, the Fleet and the Service. They are always interested and ready to help, and it keeps them well in the picture.

Once the Snottie appreciates that the Commander wants and welcomes his suggestions for the improved running of the ship, and for the comfort of the men, he produces as good ideas as anyone.

> '. . . No doubt we are different at different ages, but we cannot say that we are better; and in certain matters we can be as right at twenty as we are at sixty.'
> GOETHE, *Conversations with Eckerman,* 1831.

BIG SHIP EXECUTIVE ORGANISATION

VII.   THE FIRST AND BIGGEST EVOLUTION

COMMISSIONING DAY—A FEW NOTES

Commissioning is the first evolution with all hands, and needs to be planned down to the very smallest detail. If it goes well the effect will be lasting. First impressions are most important.

If the ship is paying off and recommissioning on the same day, it is far better to pay off the old commission in the forenoon and to start the new commission in the afternoon. If the one follows the other without an interval, the new commission is liable to make a scrambling and slovenly start in an untidy ship, and it is unlikely that a good dinner can be provided in the short time available.

It is a convenience to arrange, when possible, for certain key ratings such as cooks and supply ratings to join in advance; all such ratings should be on board by 4 P.M. on the day before paying off.

The objective on commissioning day is to settle all hands as comfortably as possible in their new home—don't try to do too much. Pray for a fine day.

TIME-TABLE

0900.   *Ship Pays off.*
When the old commission has gone, tidy up with hands recommissioning, or, if they are insufficient, keep a small retard party. Place all the guiding notices and directing arrows for the new commission.

1100.   *Rehearsal of Recommissioning Procedure.*
Required on the jetty: all Officers of Divisions, M.A.A., Chief Boatswain's Mate, Captains of Tops and all Chief and Petty Officers of the new commission already on board.

1400.   *Ship Recommissions.*
Drafts.—Drafts will be coming from all over the port; try to arrange with the various establishments to synchronise their arrival at the ship.
Embarkation.—Extra brows will be needed and should be placed in relation to the position of the messdeck hatches.
Baggage.—Arrange for the baggage of the main draft from depot to be loaded in accordance with the embarkation plan.

Baggage party to be formed from men recommissioning. Unload bags and hammocks on arrival of lorries.

Arrange alternative fair and foul weather positions for laying out bags and hammocks in groups, close to the embarkation positions, according to ships from which ratings were drafted. Position of group to be marked with the ship's name.

Bags to be stacked two high only.

Hammocks to be stacked near but separate.

Commissioning Cards.—Each department should issue its own cards.

After receiving his card, each man informs the R.P.O., at the table by the brow, whether he is 'Grog' or 'Temperance.'

Falling in by Divisions.—Men are then to fall in by Divisions:

(*a*) Fair weather: on the jetty.

(*b*) Foul weather: inboard, under awnings or other cover.

In either case the position of falling in to be marked by notices.

Procedure for Divisions.—When each Division has been mustered, the Officer of the Division will take charge and arrange for his men to do the following:

(*a*) Take bags below and place by lockers.

(*b*) Take hammocks below.

(*c*) Sling hammocks (lashed) in sleeping billets (triced well up to the beams).

(*d*) Stow kit and gas masks in their respective lockers. Each man's kit locker and gas mask locker to be marked with a number corresponding to the number on his commissioning card.

One-way Traffic Routes.—To avoid congestion on the brows, ladders and in gangways, one-way traffic routes should be used for going to and from the jetty and messdecks, and clearly marked with arrows:

(*a*) Red arrows: 'IN.'

(*b*) Green arrows: 'OUT.'

Guides.—Post guides as necessary at top and foot of ladders to direct traffic.

On Completion of Stowage.—As each man completes the above stowage he is to sit down in his mess.

Officers of Divisions report to the Commander when completed, having explained to their men the positions for falling in on the upper deck when 'Divisions' is next sounded.

Divisions.—When all Officers of Divisions have reported, sound off 'Divisions'; hands fall in on the upper deck.

Everyone in the ship is to fall in except men actually on watch.

Close Aft: Captain's Address.—Divisions close aft as soon as all are reported. The Captain addresses the ship's company.

Future Programme.—If possible a brief outline of the ship's programme after commissioning should be given. 'Clear Lower Deck' bugle to be sounded for information.

Seamen and Royal Marines.—Seamen and Royal Marines stand fast on the Quarterdeck, and the remainder march off and act under their heads of departments.

Mustering by the Watch Bill.—Seamen and Royal Marines to be mustered by the Watch Bill as follows:

(*a*) *Fall in by Parts of Watch of Hands on the Quarterdeck.*—Bugle calls for Watch of Hands and Part of Watch of Hands are sounded for information.

(*b*) *Muster Standing Parties and Power Boats' Crews.*—All Standing Parties, *vide* excused list, to be fallen out, and mustered amidships.

Bugle calls for Watch and Part of Watch to be sounded for information.

The Commander will read the following day's programme to seamen and Royal Marines.

Drawing Mess Traps.—Cooks of Messes to draw mess traps from a prearranged position.

Tea.—While hands are at tea, Commander will go round the messdecks and receive reports from Officers of Divisions that messing, stowage and sleeping billets are correct.

All men are to remain seated until the Commander has passed.

After Tea.—When the Commander is satisfied that all hands are settled, the following is to be ordered:

(*a*) Stow hammocks.

(*b*) Duty Part of the Watch to Fire Stations—read stations and then exercise.

(*c*) Leave is piped.

Fire Party from 0900 *till after Tea.*—A special fire party to be provided for this period from hands of the old commission who are recommissioning.

Watch-keepers of New Commission.—These to take over when the Duty Part of Watch of Hands falls in after tea.

Guard and W.R.A.'s.—By arrangement with Royal Marine Headquarters the necessary R.M. ratings of the old commission can be retained on board for guard and wardroom duties until after tea, when they should be disembarked.

Magazine Temperatures.—Ratings detailed from old commission should take magazine temperatures on commissioning day.

Men Recommissioning.—Men of the old commission, who are recommissioning, to sling their hammocks (lashed and well triced up) immediately after dinner.

Medical Inspection.—Medical inspection of ratings joining, to commence with Engine Room Department immediately after tea and continue next day with other departments as ordered.

Officers' Stations

Commander . .	In general charge.
All Officers and Mid-shipmen of Divisions	With their Divisions.
Lieut.-Commander .	In charge of embarkation forward.
Lieut.-Commander .	In charge of embarkation amidships.
Lieut.-Commander .	In charge of embarkation aft.
Sub - Lieutenant or Gunner . . .	Officer of the Watch.
Comd. Gunner . .	Magazines.
Three Warrant Officers	In charge of baggage parties.

Day after Commissioning

A.M.—*Quarters Clean Guns.*

Hands to fall in at their quarters, be mustered, then carry on cleaning.

Clear Lower Deck.

All hands aft. Commander explains the 'Ten Commandments.'

P.M.—*Exercise General Fire Stations.*

Second Day after Commissioning

Exercise Collision Stations.

Note.—General Quarters should be exercised preferably on the first day at sea, when all hands are on board, boats hoisted, and awnings furled.

VIII. THE COMMANDER'S OFFICE

Previous Practice.—Until quite recently it was the customary practice of the Commander of a ship to send out his Night Order Books after rounds, to tell all concerned whether or not it would be usual routine the next day, and giving the time at which he was to be called in the morning. On such meagre information, the likelihood of what the new day would bring forth must inevitably have remained a matter of guess-work for the majority of the ship's company.

Under the same system, all the work connected with the Watch Bill and the regulating of the hands was carried out by the Master-at-Arms and a large force of ship's police working from their own office. There was no broad-based Divisional system as it is now known, but only a narrow organisation which was over-centralised in the person of the Commander. The Executive Officers and the part-of-ship Petty Officers were denied a share in the task of organising and regulating the hands.

Object of the Commander's Office.—A complete change has been made since those days, and the Commander is now served by a properly organised office, which handles all the regulating work of the executive department. Discipline, and the coming and going of men to and from the ship, whether on draft or on leave, still remain in the province of the Master-at-Arms and the Regulating Petty Officers.

The main duty of the Commander's Office in the Divisional system is to act as a controlling source from which work is decentralised to the Divisions, each Division having its own office organisation.

Functions of the Commander's Office.—The functions of the Commander's Office are ten in number. (Ten seems to be the magic figure in organisation.) These functions are:

(*a*) To maintain the Seamen's Watch Bill.

(*b*) To co-ordinate the Divisional Offices.

(*c*) To regulate the employment of the hands for working parties through the Divisional Offices.

(*d*) To arrange for training classes in conjunction with the Training Officer.

(*e*) To keep the Commander's Diary of all forthcoming events.

(*f*) To draft and publish a Weekly Programme.

(*g*) To draft and publish Commander's Daily Orders.

(*h*) To promulgate information on every matter of interest to the ship's company, connected with the Service and with sport.

(*i*) To keep the Station Bill up to date.

(*j*) To circulate orders and papers to everyone concerned.

Commander's Office Staff.—The staff of the Commander's Office should be a carefully chosen team composed of the following:

1. *Lieutenant-Commander* (*R.*).—'R.' stands for Regulating; also for Right-hand.

He is the Commander's right-hand man and supervises all his office organisation. In so doing he relieves him of an immense amount of detail, attention to which would unduly absorb a Commander's time. Organisation is only a part of the work of running the ship, but it must be in capable hands.

The running of the office should be given to an able officer, who can be left to run it on his own lines, subject, of course, to a general guiding hand from the man who is responsible for executive policy.

2. *Chief Petty Officer (R.).*—He is the king of the Seamen's Watch Bill, working in close co-operation with the Chief Gunner's Mate and with the Chief Torpedo Gunner's Mate.

Under Lieutenant-Commander (R.) he co-ordinates the Divisional Offices and regulates requirements for hands.

(See Part II for method of detailing parties.)

3. *The Writer.*—The Commander's Writer plays a big part in the smooth working of the organisation. His work does not end with typing out the daily programmes and notices. If the right man is selected, he acquires knowledge of all things which may assist the efficient functioning of the ten requirements referred to above.

4. *The Messenger.*—The fourth of a small but influential team.

Promulgation of Information.—There are two instruments by means of which the Commander and his staff set out to tell the ship what is going to happen:

(*a*) *Weekly Programme.*—This consists of a day-by-day summary of all the principal events in the ship's life, forecasted for the coming week.

It is issued on Sunday, on a sheet with a printed heading.

(*b*) *Commander's Daily Orders.*—The second instrument of information and the most important is the 'Commander's Daily Orders.'

These appear in a comprehensive news sheet issued every evening from the office, giving a detailed time-table of events forecasted for the following day, and indicating any departures from normal routine.

People like to know what is happening, and the more they can be told, the better.

Lieutenant-Commander (R.) and his staff draft the Daily Orders, referring the draft to the Commander for approval, and the office then produces and issues them with a wide circulation.

Commander's 'IN' Basket.—If the Commander is wise he will on no account have an IN basket in his cabin, but he will keep it in his office, under the direct control of the office staff. The Writer then brings up the papers that concern him, at a convenient time daily. An IN basket in the cabin quickly gets littered up with every kind of paper, important and unimportant, and becomes a nuisance. The Commander of a ship should keep as clear of paper work as he can.

The Commander and his Office.—In a modern big ship, with endless calls on time, hands, boats, and an infinite variety of requirements for work and play, the Commander would be nowhere without the support of an efficient office.

His part is to keep his office fully informed of all that he knows and of all that he wants.

IX.   PUBLICITY

The Need for Commander's Notice Boards. — An up-to-date and reliable information service is essential in a big ship. Certain immediate items can be passed by 'pipe,' but there are a great many others best published by notice.

The Requirements. — The Commander needs two, or possibly three, large and serviceable notice boards, as described below, to be prominently mounted in specially selected positions, either where the hands congregate for smoking or else near a much-used gangway. It is no use issuing endless copies of typed sheets to be put up all round the ship — the notice boards get overcrowded and few trouble to read them. It is as well if one of the Commander's boards is in the vicinity of the position in which the hands fall in, as the Executive Officers then have the opportunity to glance at it daily.

Notice Boards—specifications:

> Glass doors and locking.
> Corticene back for drawing pins.
> Internal lighting.
> Board neatly subdivided with white tape.
> Size as requisite, but probably equivalent to 12 or 16 foolscap notices.
> Mounted at the correct level for the normal height of eye.
> Marked 'Commander's Notice Boards.'

Organisation:

> Glass front cleaned by messenger daily.
> No unauthorised person to have the key.
> Directly a notice is out of date, down it comes.
> Certain notices of permanent or recurring nature to have their marked billets.

These include:

> Commander's Daily Orders.
> Weekly Programme.
> Programme of Cruise.
> Liberty Boat Routine.
> Mail Routine.
> Sporting fixtures.

In addition to the above, information on all and every matter of interest to the ship's company must be promptly posted. Every paper and signal that goes to the Commander's Office should be looked at in the light of the question, is it of interest to the ship's company? If so, then the office makes the necessary notice at once.

Catching the Eye.—In this age of colourful advertisement and head-lined news, the long-winded typewritten notice is no good for catching the eye of the ship's company. The notices must be in the fewest possible words.

Give them arresting headings.

Use colours—chalks or inks—to attract the eye and to add to the gaiety of notices: red, blue, green, brown, yellow and black. At all costs avoid the drab and the dull.

The Ship's Company.—Impress on all hands at the beginning of the commission, and subsequently on newly joined men, that to be up to date and well informed they must make a habit of glancing at one of the Commander's Boards every day, and that they will never find an out-of-date notice.

To be well informed is reassuring; it checks rumour and it makes for general contentment.

H.M.S. *HOOD*—WEEKLY PROGRAMME

Week commencing ———————193— .

| | (Clean Ship) | | | | | (Training Period) | | |
| | A | B | C | D | I | II | III | IV |
	0600–0700 Scrub Decks	0800–0830 Clean Guns	0830–0900 Clean Messdecks	0900–0930 Divisions	0930–1030	1040–1110	1315–1420	1430–1540
Monday								
Tuesday								
Wednesday								
Thursday								
Friday								
Saturday					CLEAN	SHIP		

X. PLANNING THE WEEK'S WORK

With careful planning it is possible to work in together a great many of the varied requirements of training and maintenance in a big ship.

If the line is taken that only one activity at a time is possible, much will never get done. But if at the weekly meeting of the Executive Officers, for which Saturday is usually the best day, all the work on the upper deck for the coming week is planned ahead, it is surprising how many things are easily fitted in.

The officers come prepared to state all their requirements for 'G.' and 'T.' drills and practices, working parties, training classes, and any other items shown in the Commander's Diary.

The form shown opposite has been used with advantage; it provides useful and clear subdivision for fitting in the day's work.

First of all comes the 'Clean Ship' rectangle, which encloses the period from 0600 to 0900 daily; this appears also in the Excused List (see Part II).

The Commander must watch like a dragon to preserve the integrity of periods A, B and C in his precious rectangle. But if all hands have worked together with a will to clean the ship completely by Divisions, then for the rest of the day it is possible to give up the majority of the time to training and maintenance.

Training includes:

> 'G.' and 'T.' Drills and Practices.
> General Drills and Landing Parties.
> Acting 'G.' and 'T.' Training Classes.
> Advancement Classes for Petty Officer and Leading
>   Seaman.
> Ordinary Seamen's and Boys' Training Classes.
> Boys' School Classes.
> Any other drills and training.

Maintenance includes:

> Part of Ship Refitting and Repair Work.
> Cleaning of Paintwork and Preparing Surfaces.
> Storing and Provisioning.

Training Periods.—After Divisions the day is conveniently divided into four equal parts, giving twenty periods in the week. Even during the most intensive programme of armament drills or practices, barely half of this number should be needed for 'G.' and 'T.,' provided the week's work is planned out ahead. By this means, instead of in advance dismissing a week as 'all Gunnery,' the Commander finds that there is time over to make steady and often surprising progress in other forms of training, especially with classes for ordinary seamen and boys. There is also time to fit in the ceaseless storing and provisioning required for a floating population of over one thousand men.

Working Parties.—The Commander is often told that unless some storing party or other commences its work directly after breakfast, it will not get finished that day. Very reluctantly he allows an inroad into his 'Clean Ship' rectangle, and he duly finds that the party finishes about 1540. One day he puts his foot down and refuses to let a working party go till after Divisions, only to find that, mysteriously, it still finishes at 1540. After that he is firm.

With practice the Executive Team is able to forecast a week's work with considerable accuracy, and this results in a substantial increase of efficiency in training and maintenance.

XI. TURNING OUT WITH THE HANDS

It has been said that the traditional practice of the Commander turning out with the hands in the early morning, to start them off with the order to scrub and wash the upper deck, is old-fashioned and illogical, and more than once the purpose which he serves by so doing has been called in question.

An Army officer who travelled home in one of H.M. ships from Malta stated that nothing on board amazed him more than to see the Commander of the ship, corresponding in rank to a Lieutenant-Colonel, coming on deck at six o'clock in the morning to do the job which the Sergeant-Major does in barracks, and which no one above him would dream of doing for him.

Traditional practices are seldom easy to defend on any but sentimental grounds, but it is believed that, in this case, there are definite and solid reasons for the Commander being there when the hands turn-to first thing.

He stands in a special and unique position in regard to his hands, and in his mind's eye there should always be a continuous and up-to-date picture of their work and of the routine. If he is not up at the start of the day, he will never have the same grasp as the Commander who makes it his duty to be there.

And if he is not there at the beginning, how is he to appreciate the conditions for scrubbing decks on cold, dark and wet mornings or in rough weather? If on such occasions the Commander, in deciding to give a lie-in to the hands, is also giving one to himself, he is far less likely to overlook the occasions when such indulgence is justified and necessary, as it not infrequently is. In any case, an occasional change of routine is good for all, but the moments for it are unlikely to be well chosen by a man asleep in his bunk.

The Commander of the Senior Officer's ship or of a single ship has to decide the most suitable dress for the day, before the hands go to breakfast and clean. There again he must be on deck himself.

There is no need for other officers to support him, excepting those on watch. He can manage quite well on his own.

Scrubbing decks is not everyone's choice of occupation at 0600, but the Commander's presence every morning makes all the difference.

'Carry on, Sergeant-Major' is not good enough.

XII.   STARTING WORK BY STOP-WATCH

Loss of Time.—Lack of method in telling off the hands is a most fruitful source of loss of time and work.

Many of us must have served in ships in which it has usually taken five minutes for the hands to arrive, and another five or even more to tell them off—ten minutes lost on every man's work, and a slack and slovenly start which is sure to mean further loss.

Losing ten minutes' work with 200 men is equivalent to losing a dozen men for the whole afternoon.

Telling off the Hands.—A straightforward and simple procedure on which to insist from the beginning of the commission is required:

(1) *'G'* (on bugle).—Sounded ten minutes before the hands are due to fall in for work. This warns all hands to make a move towards the falling-in place.

(2) *'Out Pipes'* (on bugle and pipe). *'Boys fall in.'*—Five minutes before falling in; warns all hands that they should now be at their falling-in place, and also not to light up again—they may finish off what they are smoking.

(3) *'Hands fall in'* (on bugle).—All hands are to fall in at once. No straggling is allowed: first time late gets a warning from the Captain of Top, second time late goes in report.

The Commander should have a fixed rendezvous at 'Out Pipes' with all those requiring hands, so that, directly they have fallen in and have been reported to him correct by the Chief Boatswain's Mate, he can tell them off without any delay.

It is suggested that the Commander's Messenger should carry a stop-watch, which he starts with the bugle to fall in, and he stops the watch as 'Carry on, Captains of Tops' is finally ordered; the total time taken need not exceed one minute, and should usually be under 45 seconds.

Telling off the hands is a matter of careful planning and stage management, and there is always room for improvement; the trouble taken is well repaid.

To muster each man by name every time of falling in causes delay in getting on with the work. It is simpler to cover off in fours and to let the Captains of Tops count the number present. An occasional roll-call made without warning, and a wary eye on the part of the Petty Officer in charge of each messdeck, soon reveals the skulker; a dose of 'No. 11' quickly cures him and serves as a warning to others.

The three principal musters of the hands for work during the day are items of major importance in the Commander's time-table. Unfailing punctuality and the necessary mental concentration are required of him, to enable the foregoing procedure to be carried out successfully. It happens, too often, that he will be summoned elsewhere, or that his attention will be otherwise distracted, just at the time when he should be arriving at his rendezvous for telling off the hands. Other calls must wait, or, if he cannot possibly be present, then the officer next in seniority must carry on in his place without waiting.

XIII.   WARMING THE BELL

Stopping Work Punctually.—If all hands start work punctually and together, they should also finish punctually and together. Those who work in Standing Parties and Sweepers are apt to find themselves sitting in their messes soon after 'Secure' is sounded, if not before.

To stop this, give the offender an extra afternoon's work at the next make-and-mend; the punishment fits the crime—it is the growth of the disease of cutting corners which endangers the policy of making-and-mending clothes with regularity.

If it recurs with men of the same standing party, cut down the strength of the party, and this will stir those in charge to stricter supervision.

Once 'Cooks' has been sounded, men may be sent away as they finish off their work.

Smoking should not be allowed to start until the meal is piped. To make this clear the order to carry on smoking can be passed by bugle and pipe after piping the meal.

XIV.   STARTING LEAVE PUNCTUALLY

If punctuality in falling in and starting work is insisted on, and if no cutting of corners at the end of work is permitted, then it is only fitting that the organisation to ensure that leave starts punctually and comfortably shall be equally thorough.

It must never happen that the libertymen are standing about, perhaps in the rain, waiting for their boat to come alongside, or waiting to be inspected.

For the main liberty boats the team of Duty Officers, Petty Officers and N.C.O.'s should be on deck, and the boats ready manned at the gangways, before the libertymen fall in.

Disembarking Libertymen as an Evolution.—Falling in, checking, inspecting and disembarking libertymen should be one of the ship's smartest evolutions.

When lying alongside, a big ship should be able to perform the evolution, from the first bugle to the last man stepping off, in less than five minutes with over 700 libertymen.

It is just a matter of organisation and team work.

Leave cards are now in general use and save an immense amount of time and shouting of names.

Consideration for Libertymen.—The utmost consideration is due to libertymen: proper protection from weather on deck and in the boats—adequate boats—no unnecessary waiting about at either end. Before being piped to fall in, they should be warned if the Officer of the Watch considers it advisable to take oilskins.

If the Commander uses a stop-watch to see how quickly he can get work started, that same stop-watch should be in operation for starting leave, especially at home ports.

Liberty Boats—Routine.—There are certain determining factors in the arrangement of a convenient routine of boats for libertymen. The conditions of ship life make it desirable to facilitate shore-going for the sake of healthy exercise, for a change of scene, and for a variation in the routine of life.

A man can usually go ashore while his money lasts. The longer it lasts, the longer he can keep on going. That will not be for long if, in addition to going to the pictures, to the canteen, to a football match, or for a walk, he has also to buy his meals. The boat routine can have a decisive influence on this point, if it is compiled in direct relation to those meals which are served on board during the time that leave is being given. If a man can come off for a meal, or if he can land after having his meal on board, he will save money, and he is, in consequence, likely to be able to take a run ashore more frequently. He can also land for a couple of hours' walk in the afternoon, and come off for his tea.

When, for example, leave is given from 1300 to 0700, liberty boats are required as follows:

> 1300.   Land libertymen.
> Before tea (about 1600).   Bring off libertymen.
> After tea (about 1645).   Land libertymen.
> Before supper (about 1830).   Bring off libertymen.
> After supper (about 1930).   Land libertymen.
> 2200.   Bring off libertymen.
> 2330.   Bring off libertymen.

Note.—(1) The boats before and after tea and supper can, of course, carry libertymen both ways, the main purpose only of the trips being shown above.

(2) A routine of liberty boats, as distinct from the general boat routine of the ship, should be published on the Commander's Notice Boards.

. . . Foul Weather Routine . . .

XV.   NOTES ON ROUTINES

To settle the ship down, a regular and punctual routine is necessary. Regularity is required in the sense that major items are not changed about without very good reason, and strict punctuality in the timing adds to the general comfort and convenience. If, for example, the times of meals or stand-easy vary by even a few minutes from day to day, an atmosphere of uncertainty is created, which in turn leads to the vice of 'warming the bell.'

The routine should never be held up while someone is trying to find the Commander. Certain times are reported to him, solely with the idea of keeping him in the picture. But the routine must go forward like clockwork unless he has actually ordered a change, in which case the necessary word of warning should be passed in good time.

Change of Routine.—A complete change of routine occasionally is good for everyone and relieves monotony. In this way General Drill, Landing Parties and General Quarters all help, and, by bringing the between-deck workers up into the light of day for a temporary change of occupation, they do good to health.

Making-and-Mending of Clothes.—Training classes should work during the mid-week make-and-mend when given, and get their half-day on Saturdays with the remainder. This rule adheres to the principle that when a man is under training for higher rating, he is working for his own advantage as well as that of the Service, and he should therefore make some contribution from his own time to the week's work.

Foul Weather Routine.—No good purpose is served by falling men in at 0600 on a wild and wet morning, and possibly also in the dark and cold, to scrub the decks, either at sea or in harbour. It is wiser to wait for daylight, when the elements are better faced by men who have already breakfasted.

A foul weather routine is thus needed, with discretionary power for the Officer of the Morning Watch to change over when he thinks it necessary, at the same time informing the Commander.

The routine is briefly as follows:

0600.	Call the hands.
0645.	Breakfast.
0730.	Hands fall in. Scrub decks.

Not much time is lost. By 0800 the routine is only half an hour behind, and this is made up by taking ten minutes from each of the 'Clean ship' items—the upper deck, the guns and the messdecks. The loss of time is more than compensated for by the advantages gained from this routine, in the consideration it shows for the men, as well as a welcome variation in the performance of the least congenial task in the day's work.

Routine after Hours.—'Staysail Jack' was the name given in the old days to the type of officer who was for ever piping 'Set Staysail' or 'Down Staysail,' for no apparent reason but to disturb the men. To obtain ready support in emergency, it is essential to study how to avoid disturbing men unnecessarily during quiet times. It should be laid down as axiomatic for 'Routine after hours' that:

(*a*) The watch below is never to be disturbed except for emergency.

(*b*) The non-duty part of the watch on deck is to be used as little as possible.

(c) When leave is given, men who might if they chose have been ashore should never be called on except in emergency, from after Evening Quarters until hands fall in the next morning.

If these rules are faithfully observed, a man has the chance to feel a sense of peace and security in his leisure time on board, and to think of his ship as his home. On the other hand, if leave is piped to the watch and, two hours later, *both* watches are fallen in for the routine hoisting of boats, men will be driven out of the ship to escape from disturbance.

Mornings at Home Ports.—When at home ports and with all night leave to the watch and part, it will be found of little use to try to scrub the decks with only a quarter of the hands at 0600.

In the winter especially it becomes a farce—water is swilled over decks which are neither properly scrubbed nor properly dried, due to lack of hands, and the result is a muddy and sodden deck. In consequence, a morning routine at home port is required, similar to that for foul weather:

0600.	Call the hands.
0645.	Breakfast.
0700.	Leave expires.
0730.	Hands fall in.

Breakfast being at 0645 encourages punctuality among libertymen, and at 0730 work starts with all hands. A routine on these lines proves its value beyond question in contributing both to cleanliness and contentment.

It reduces the amount of sleeping on shore by non-natives, and here again helps to make the ship more of a home, rather than a place of duty only. Sleeping on board saves money for long leave or for more frequent shore-going, which is all for the good of those leading the abnormal and crowded life of a ship.

Running the Routine.—The Ship's Routine is a special province of the Midshipman of the Watch, assisted by the Leading Hand of the Watch. They require a well-situated and adequately equipped headquarters from which to do their work. It must be central, protected from weather, with good notice boards, on the telephone; it must have a convenient table, a reliable clock, and must be in direct communication with the Commander and the gangway.

Adjusting the Routine.—So much depends on the smooth working of the routine that it calls for a very close study until the requirements of the ship and the station have been met in every detail.

XVI.   THE SEVENTH DAY

'The ship's company is not to be employed on Sundays in any work or duty other than that which may be strictly necessary for the public service.'—King's Regulation.

There is no doubt that—

(1) A weekly day of rest is desirable and reasonable.
(2) A change of routine is good for all hands.

Normal Sunday Routine.—The normal Sunday Routine on the upper deck is far from being a day of rest and change, from early morning until mid-day. It opens with 'Usual Daily Routine—¼ hour late.' Turning the hands out at 0545 to scrub the deck instead of turning them out at 0530 to do the same work, is a negligible concession, and, by crowding 'Scrub Decks' into a shorter time, the day starts off with a scramble from which it does not recover until dinner is piped at noon.

It may be suggested that it is necessary to keep the hands on the go, in case they should not know what to do with their leisure. This can be disproved by the fact that other branches in the ship contrive to look on contentedly, while their brethren of the upper deck rush from scrub decks to breakfast; to clean guns; to clean messdecks and bright work on the upper deck; to clean themselves; to Divisions; to rig church; to church; to unrig church; and finally, after six hours on the go, at long last to dinner. Other departments in the ship enjoy what is virtually a complete stand-off, from noon on Saturday until turn-to on Monday, except for presenting themselves properly dressed at Sunday Divisions.

The atmosphere resulting from such a routine denies any possibility of Sunday seeming a day of rest and quiet, and the accusation may justly be laid at the Executive door of having spoiled the day for the Padre.

Routine at the Week-end.—Experiments were carried out, and a routine evolved, in which the work is so arranged that all hands are given a quieter Sunday.

Broadly speaking, the cleaning of the ship, together with the Captain's rounds of the messdecks and flats on Saturday fore-noon, are followed by Divisions and the customary inspection of the ship's company and the upper deck, as for Sunday. So much having been fitted into Saturday, it is easy enough to improve on Sunday's routine.

With careful organisation of deck cloths, roping off little-used parts of the deck, and with the co-operation of the ship's company, it was found unnecessary to scrub the decks on Sunday. This enables an important and much-appreciated change in routine to be made, all hands turning out with guard and steerage; breakfast is at 0700 and is followed by the necessary cleaning of the living quarters, clearing up decks, and a quick polish of the bright work on the upper deck and at the guns.

If proper care is taken, the deck suffers very little over the week-end, some work with a mop being needed here and there, and, in actual fact, the deck looks generally better and whiter from being left dry for once.

The hands are piped to clean at the usual time on Sunday and then to carry on smoking.

The salient features of this Saturday–Sunday Routine are as follows:

Saturday.

Until 1000.	Clean ship as usual.
1020.	Captain's Rounds of the messdecks and flats.
1050.	Clear up decks for Divisions.
1110.	Hands to clean for Divisions.
1125.	Hands to Divisions.
1200.	Dinner.
	Make and mend clothes.

Experience has shown that it would be preferable to carry out Messdecks Rounds on some other day of the week, such as Friday, to avoid overcrowding of Saturday's routine. It is possible to fit it in as above, but rounds have to be rather hurried in a large ship.

Sunday.

0615.	Call all hands with Guard and Steerage.
0700.	Breakfast.
0745.	Clean guns.
0810.	Clean messdecks.
	Clear up the upper deck. Rig church.
0910.	Hands to clean.
0930.	Clear off the messdecks. Carry on smoking.
	Church.
	Pipe Down.

This routine works well and is welcomed by everyone. Better work is produced during the week, because the hands, in common with the general run of their fellow-countrymen, have a day of peace and quiet to look forward to on Sunday.

The Advantages of Saturday Divisions.—Apart from the reason for which the change was first conceived, 'Saturday Divisions' has been found to possess other advantages:

(*a*) More men attend, as no Church Parties are away. Normally up to a hundred men and more are never seen by the Captain from this cause. A big ship has as many as two hundred men of other religious denominations.

(*b*) The number of libertymen landing on Saturday is increased. This is the most cheerful night in any place, as the world comes out shopping with the week's wages, and it is the most popular night to go ashore. But due to Sunday routine casting its shadow, and to the necessary preparations of kit for Sunday Divisions, many men do not normally land on Saturday. With the Royal Marines especially, it is one of the smallest leave nights of the week.

From the point of view of service efficiency alone, it is clearly desirable to facilitate shore-going on a night which is not followed by a working day, apart from the natural wish to make it easy for the men to go ashore when they will get most enjoyment.

(*c*) It seems a more fitting climax to the working week for the Captain to complete all his inspections by noon on Saturday. If the ship is not clean by that time, Sunday is hardly the right day on which to make up leeway.

(*d*) It is also very well suited to time spent in home ports, where week-end leave is given. 'Saturday Divisions' then has the double advantage of providing for the essential requirement that the Captain should inspect all hands once a week and, in addition, those who are going on leave on Saturday afternoon are cleaned in 'Number Ones' in good time for landing.

Conclusion.—The experiments have shown that officers and men like the routine and look forward to it at the end of the week's work. Apart from going to church, Sunday is spent in writing, reading, smoking, talking, sleeping, thinking, sitting in the sun (if any), or in doing nothing at all. As evidence of these activities, the issue of library books advanced by more than 30 per cent. to a total of over three hundred on Sundays, while the sale of postage stamps was also increased, when the routine was in use.

'. . . SATURDAY NIGHT ASHORE . . .'

Summary of Advantages.—The advantages of a Saturday–Sunday routine as here described can be summarised as follows:

(*a*) It conforms with the Law of Moses ('Six days shalt thou labour . . .').

(*b*) It conforms with the letter and the spirit of the King's Regulations.

(*c*) It conforms with age-old English custom and practice.

(*d*) It gives the Padre a fair field.

(*e*) It adds to the contentment of every person on board.

XVII. HAMMOCKS AND BREAKFAST

Every hammock in the ship should be lashed up and stowed by 0645 on every morning of the commission, including Sunday and not excluding anyone; this order should be on every messdeck and enclosed mess.

The rule must be rigidly enforced, and the O.O.W. or Midshipman of the Watch with the Duty R.P.O. should make the rounds at that time.

It is bad enough for a man to have to turn out and scrub the decks at six o'clock in the morning, but it is still worse if when he comes down to breakfast he finds someone from Guard and Steerage just getting out of a hammock slung over the mess table, and getting mixed up with his breakfast.

It is unpleasant and causes unpleasantness.

Offences against this order should go to the Commander: first time a caution; second time, for Leading Rates and above, a few days' leave stopped; others, a minor punishment such as two days' No. 16.

A strict rule on this matter contributes in no small measure to the comfort of life on the messdecks.

XVIII.   PART OF SHIP AND MESS CHANGES

Care is needed to ensure that a man's part of ship and his mess are never changed unless it is absolutely necessary, or for some good reason it is to his advantage. Quarrelling and mutual antipathies sometimes make a change desirable, and cases occur when a fresh start in a new environment and with different associates will turn a youngster from wrong ways.

Changes should be made only through the Officer of Division, all changes finally receiving the Commander's authority.

A man cannot feel settled at his work, nor will he feel at home in his mess and among his messmates, if he lives constantly under the threat of being moved, in order to satisfy the exact and mathematical balancing of the Watch Bill or Quarter Bill. He cannot feel a real interest in the success of his part of ship at work and play, or in the cleanliness of his mess and quarters, in such an atmosphere of uncertainty.

The executive policy must aim at reducing changes to a minimum, and the reason for a change, when it has been proved inevitable, needs to be fully explained to the individual concerned by his Divisional Officer.

It causes very considerable disturbance in a man's life if he is suddenly uprooted and put down again among strange topmates and with new messmates, and each change may well disturb many more than the one man.

The Quarter Bill at times lays claim to absolute rights over the individual, demanding abrupt changes which tend to ignore the need for his considerate treatment. The Commander constitutes the Court of Appeal, and he will almost always be able to arrive at a compromise which satisfies the requirements both of fighting efficiency and of the humanities.

THE SHIP'S AIR ARM

XIX. EXECUTIVE ORGANISATION FOR THE AIR ARM

General Note.—The Air Arm is an integral part of the modern big ship and, as such, demands its own section of the executive organisation. Ship-borne aircraft are not fragile toys to be handled only by a specially trained personnel of standing numbers: the organisation for handling them should be on a watch and part of watch basis, as employed for hoisting boats, weighing anchor, and other evolutions.

Air Division.—The Air Division comprises all officers and men of the Royal Navy and Royal Air Force borne for duty with the ship's Air Arm; the total strength of the division when a flight is carried is between twenty and thirty. Observer officers have other divisions in the ship, being part of the upper deck complement.

Organisation of Air Division.—In Part II of this book, under the heading of 'Air Division,' will be found full details of the establishment, and of the executive organisation required for the Air Arm.

The following notes may help to elucidate various points arising in considering the needs of a flight of aircraft in a big ship.

(*a*) *Messing.*—Although the Air Division consists of men from two services, it is more efficient for working as a unit if they mess together. They do this when disembarked to a Royal Air Force station.

N.C.O. Airmen of Sergeant's rank should mess with the Royal Marine sergeants, or if this is not possible, with the Petty Officers. A Flight-Sergeant R.A.F. ranks with a Chief Petty Officer.

(*b*) *Discipline and Leave.*—The Air Division is administered through the Master-at-Arms' Office for leave and disciplinary matters.

(*c*) *Routine for Airmen.*—An airman is a skilled tradesman, and at Royal Air Force stations no routine work is carried out before breakfast; a suggested routine is included in Part II.

(*d*) *Duty Air Party.*—The Air Division should be divided into watches and parts of watch, so that there is always an Air Party in the duty part of the watch, during non-working hours.

(*e*) *Action Stations.*—The primary action station for aircraft crews is at their aircraft, but they should be given secondary stations for occasions when they are not required for flying. The maintenance personnel will be required for handling and catapulting aircraft, but should be given an additional action station in supply or repair parties.

Aircraft Stores.—All naval and R.A.F. stores and spares supplied to the ship come under the Central Storekeeping Officer, who has a supply rating qualified in R.A.F. stores procedure on his staff, and these stores are issued to the flight for use in the ordinary way. The aircraft and all flight equipment are on the charge of the Flight Commander.

'. . . Ship's Air Arm . . .'

XX. HANDLING AIRCRAFT IN A BIG SHIP

(*a*) *Personnel.*—On recommissioning, or during initial trials after first installation of a catapult and aircraft, it is necessary to have specially trained crews for the catapult and aircraft handling parties, and these same crews must obviously be chosen, so that the catapult will be their primary action station. However, as soon after commissioning as possible, catapult and aircraft handling crews should be trained from each part of the watch, as aircraft are liable to be required at any time of the day; the working-up period will be a suitable time for training this personnel, which includes officers as well as men.

(*b*) *Boats.*—A stand-by boat is always required to be in attendance when aircraft are being operated, and the following is suggested:

> *In harbour.*—A power boat lying off the ship, and to be down wind of the aircraft taking off.
> *At sea.*—A sea-boat to be manned and ready for lowering.

The following should always go away in the stand-by boat:

A salvage officer.
Sick berth attendant with stretcher and medical bag.
A F.A.A. rating with salvage gear and crash box.

(*c*) *Catapulting.*—A complete drill for the type fitted is issued to every ship on installation of the catapult.

(*d*) *Hoisting out.*—An aircraft is hoisted out with the engine running, and if possible should be lowered head to wind. Steadying lines are rove through suitable places in the tail and inboard wing-tip of aircraft, so that they can be slipped as requisite. A quick release coupling is fitted to the crane purchase, so that the aircraft can be slipped by one of the aircraft's crew as she touches the water.

(The procedure is similar to that of a sea-boat, but it must be remembered that an aircraft undercarriage is not so strong as a boat's hull.)

(*e*) *Hoisting in.*—Aircraft always approach in the same manner as a boat, except when the ship is secured head and stern, when the approach is head to wind; in cases of wind against tide, the direction of approach is against whichever has the more effect. The Thomas grab is fitted to the crane purchase, which enables the hook to be lowered quickly as soon as the air screw is clear; when the aircraft is hooked on the pilot stops his engine. The pilot is in charge of the aircraft until it is hooked on, when the crane officer takes over and hoists it inboard.

For hoisting aircraft, as with all seamanlike evolutions, there are several good methods of execution, and these again differ according to the type of ship. The following is a method which has been found satisfactory in a battleship:

Aircraft are fitted with small wire steadying lines which lead from the tail on either side and both wing-tips up to the centre section, where the slings are. These lines are only held in place by clips along the fuselage and wings, so that they will pull out clear when required. If two hemp lines are lowered on the crane hook, one can be attached to the wing-tip line and the other to the tail line, so that before the aircraft leaves the water it is held by the tail, wing-tip and slings. For handling the aircraft during hoisting, it is far more efficient to have the steadying lines controlled from the same place, where they can be belayed if necessary, and also worked without fouling the aircraft. To do this, the hemp parts should be led through blocks secured to the jib of the crane where suitable, and this will also allow the crane to be trained, if the lines are secured to some part of the jib.

(*f*) *Hoisting in with the Ship under way.*—This also can be done by several methods, and here again is one which has been found satisfactory in a big ship:

The aircraft taxies up alongside the ship and keeps station, underneath the crane; the purchase is lowered with quick release coupling attached, and when the pilot is satisfied he gives the order to the aircraft's crew to hook on. As soon as he has hooked on, the man holds up his hand and the crane officer immediately hoists the aircraft clear of the water; the steadying lines are rove; and the procedure is the same for hoisting in harbour. In this operation, care must be taken not to hook on or hoist when the aircraft is too much to one side or in any way astern of the crane purchase. Also it should be remembered that it is cheaper and easier to mend a wing-tip than the main planes, fuselage or engine.

(*g*) *Securing Aircraft.*—Aircraft can be made fast astern of the ship, and all that is required for this is a grass line and buoy; the aircraft will pick up the buoy and secure to the grass line.

Aircraft stowed on the catapult and deck now have spread, as well as folded type, holding-down gear, which has been proved to be adequate in the strongest gale.

(*h*) *Float-plane Trot.*—When laying out a trot, always allow plenty of sea-room all round, as aircraft cannot go astern and the wind may blow from any direction. Rubber buoys are most suitable, as aircraft floats are easily damaged.

DISCIPLINE

XXI. DEFAULTERS AND REQUESTMEN

Rule I   .   .   .   .   . Punctuality.

Rule II   .   .   .   .   . Patience.

Punctuality.—Unpunctuality by the Commander at his table is a serious failing, not only because of the great inconvenience it causes, but also because officers and petty officers in exasperation may give up reporting offenders, and discipline will suffer; worse still, men may hesitate to bring their requests up.

The Commander must have a fixed time for arrival at the table and stick to it; after telling off the hands at 0830 is suitable, and it should be possible for him to arrive punctually on every weekday of the commission, except on very few occasions, such as when the ship is leaving or entering harbour just at that time. Due notice can then be given of an altered time, or of postponement to the following day.

The Commander needs to be in a consistently judicial frame of mind for his magisterial duties, and it is most necessary for him to regulate the daily morning details of his domestic life strictly in relation to the time of his defaulters.

Requestmen.—Requestmen should not necessarily be in the dress of the day, and should be seen first.

Every request should be given careful consideration, and requestmen must feel assured of a sympathetic hearing.

If a request has to be refused, the reason should be explained and the man given the option of coming up again if he wants to, or if necessary of seeing the Captain.

Defaulters.—Defaulters should be in the dress of the day.

First Offenders Act.—The majority of small offences are committed by thoughtlessness or mischance and not by intention, and after one solemn warning most men are careful not to reappear as defaulters.

Leave-breaking.—Minor leave-breaking is inevitable and is one of the recurring problems. Not one of us is so punctual in habit, or can order his life so exactly, as never to fail to keep an appointment; accidents will happen. Every leave-breaker should go before the Commander.

Is there anyone who can still believe in the tales of the grim-faced, tight-lipped, lantern-jawed disciplinarians of legend who were wont to give the first leave-breaker of the commission 'Ninety days,' and as a result never had another? It is palpable nonsense!

Others will have their own ideas on punishing leave-breakers, but it is essential to work to a definite plan, and the following is suggested:

First offence: If reasonable explanation—Caution.
If no reasonable explanation—Scale.
Second offence: Scale.
Third offence: Captain's Report.

In every ship's company there are a very few regular leave-breakers—they will need sterner measures.

'Ten Commandments.'—In the course of a commission in a big ship, the Commander may see some three thousand defaulters. Most of the offences will be of a minor character, and all except a very few will be found to be clearly covered by one of the 'Ten Commandments.' The attention of the delinquent should always be called to the Commandment he has infringed.

Long-drawn-out punishments are seldom necessary or desirable; the Commander should see all the more serious offenders again on the conclusion of their punishment, when he may be able to give them wise counsel and to urge them to go and sin no more.

Misleading Appearances.—Appearances are often misleading, and when they are unfavourable to the accused one may be misled into an injustice. Remember the old Chinese proverb: 'A man may be a teetotaller, but if his nose is red, no one will believe it.'

Crime and Punishment.—Beccaria, the eighteenth-century reformer whose penal research work forms the main foundation of the criminal codes of civilised countries of to-day, left behind him some thoughts on crime and punishment which seem to be of unchanging application:

(1) 'Crimes are more certainly prevented by the certainty than by the severity of the punishments.'

(2) 'The countries most noted for the severity of punishments are always those in which the most bloody and inhuman actions are committed, for the hand of the assassin and of the legislator are directed by the same spirit of ferocity.'

(3) 'An immediate punishment is always the more useful.'

(4) 'Crime is often caused by the laws themselves.'

(5) 'One method of preventing crime is to reward virtue.'

'. . . Appearances are often misleading . . .'

General.—In dealing with defaulters a Commander comes face to face with an endless variety of motives and mischances which bring men to his table, cap in hand. It is a central truth of human nature that men's faults are the corollary of their virtues, and that without our faults we should be different men for good, as well as for ill. Justice is most just when tempered with mercy.

Practice makes perfect—'Defaulters' looms large in a Commander's life at first, and then gradually recedes to its proper size—

BUT

HE MUST BE PUNCTUAL.

XXII. NAGGING

'I have always considered peevish words and hasty orders detrimental, and it has been my study not to utter the one or issue the other.'

These lines were written by Lord Bridport from his flagship in the Channel Fleet at Spithead during the sad events of 1797, and show him as the determined enemy of the Nagger and of Nagging.

The tendency to nag arises from human fretfulness, and there is nothing to surpass it for making an intelligent man feel insubordinate. Injustice is far easier to put up with than any form of bully-ragging. The Commander has to make it clear early in the commission to all those set in authority under him that, no matter what is done or left undone, he will not have things aggravated by nagging.

It pushes its head up in many unexpected places. Some people have nagging voices—tell them about it, and insist on a change of voice. Others, seeing a man doing wrong, at once utter peevish words or hasty orders, instead of quietly correcting the fault—stop them.

And when the Commander himself starts nagging at the Officer of the Watch, then it is time for him to leave the Quarterdeck—it does no one any good and puts people in a flat spin.

The dignity of a great Service like ours alone requires that every officer and man shall be given credit in the first place for doing his best, and when he sins, of sinning in ignorance or from forgetfulness. Then, if he still fails, those in authority can afford to act calmly, seeing that they are backed by the authority of the whole Service and the Naval Discipline Act, with the Lords Spiritual and Temporal and all the Commons in support.

If a man is sulking, the chances are that someone has been nagging him.

All men, young and old, are sensitive and it does not do to speak roughly, or someone will be burning with indignation from a neglect of courtesy, of which you may remain profoundly unconscious.

XXIII. PETTY THEFT

The incidence of petty theft on the messdecks is a difficult and disturbing problem. It is difficult because a thief is seldom caught red-handed, and it is disturbing because it engenders an unhappy atmosphere of suspicion among messmates.

Unless he is a kleptomaniac, the man who steals from a shipmate must be the meanest of mortals. Experience shows that he is also, usually, most cunning, and, regrettably, he is seldom laid by the heels.

If ever there was a case of Prevention being better than Cure, it is so with theft. Men are very careless with their money, and they leave it about in a way which must often sorely tempt the light-fingered. Money in a belt hung from the end of a hammock while the owner sleeps, or money placed in an unlocked ditty box, are quite frequently reported among the losses. A solemn warning is needed to all hands, prominently displayed on the Commander's Notice Boards, and repeated whenever necessary, that there is no safe place for money except—

    (1) On a man's person.
    (2) Deposited with the Paymaster.

Those who disregard this warning and suffer loss have only themselves to blame, and it is up to them to catch the thief.

XXIV.   THIS 'NAME' BUSINESS

Some people appear to be specially gifted in learning and remembering the names of those with whom they serve. It is an art in which all of us would like to excel, being in a Service in which the personal factor counts for so much.

Nearly everyone feels he is bad at names and envies the few who seem to have the gift. Is it a 'gift,' however? If it is, then those without it have cause to despair. But if it is not, there is a chance for all.

I have sought the help of two or three notably successful dealers in 'names,' and, added to my own slight experience, I have formed the following opinions:

It is not a gift.

First, it is a matter of feeling strong personal interest in the individual.

Secondly, as in all other manifestations of genius, it requires the taking of pains; and here perhaps the broader definition of genius as 'one-tenth inspiration and nine-tenths perspiration' fits the case, as it combines effectively both the above points. But in its application the world must never be allowed to see the perspiration or much of the effect is spoiled.

Assuming then that it is not a gift, and that one is keen to be good at 'names' and willing to work at it, how to set about the task?

Never ask a man his name directly as a means of learning it—a subtler approach is needed; if the first time you speak to him you call him by name, he will feel that his fame must have gone before him.

Make a complete nominal list of those whose names you want to learn, properly subdivided. It may be a Division, a Watch or a whole Ship's Company. Against each name must be filled in all the details by which it may be possible to identify him: sub. and non-sub. rating, mess, action station, special duties, boat, games, and a good big 'Remarks' column.

Every time you learn a name by hearing it called, or that you identify a man by his job, make an entry the same day on your list, and add a brief description in the remarks column; at the same time trying to note down any distinctive points about his appearance.

At regular intervals go through the list to ascertain progress and record the total numbers known, against the date. The result cannot help but be encouraging. Progress will be steady and continuous if you persevere, and you will eventually improve by practice.

A certain officer tells me how he tried these methods in a big ship, determined if it were humanly possible to learn the name of every soul in her. He found that, after an initial crop of some two hundred names in the first month, he advanced steadily at the rate of about fifty a month to a total of six hundred. That seemed to be his point of saturation, and for every new name learnt an old one slipped out, and he never got much beyond the six hundred mark. But even then he seemed to know practically everyone in the ship with whom he came in contact. After leaving her, one of his old shipmates told him that the general impression had been that after a few weeks in the ship he had known the name of every man on board. He knew only too well that that was not true, but it goes to show how generously efforts may be rewarded, and thus how well worth while it is to make the effort. But once again—never let the world see one drop of the perspiration.

Until you know a man's name he has no separate identity for you. Directly you know it, a bridge is slipped across the gap and you very quickly begin to know a lot of other things too—and so will he.

Mistakes will happen! After paying off from *Royal Sovereign* I joined Whale Island, and a week later, walking round the island, met an old shipmate whose face I knew, but could not recollect his name or where we had served together in the past. I stopped and greeted him, asking where it was we had met before, and the slightly surprised, if not offended, answer was: '*Royal Sovereign,* sir'!

CLEANLINESS

XXV. KEEPING A BIG SHIP CLEAN

'It takes more work to keep a slovenly ship slovenly than it does to keep a smart ship clean.'

Two vital factors are:

(*a*) Careful organisation.

(*b*) Strong personal interest.

1. *Organisation.*—The organisation should aim at cleaning the ship thoroughly every weekday by the time of Divisions; the available time being allocated to scrubbing the decks, cleaning the guns, cleaning the messdecks and flats, and cleaning bright-work on the upper deck.

(*a*) *Excused List.*—The Excused List is as important a list as any in the ship. Who shall be excused his share in cleaning his ship? The answer is, No one, unless he can prove an irrefutable claim to be employed in other work.

Much care is needed in making out the Excused List—a specimen is given in Part II of this book.

The left-hand section of the table, which is clearly delineated, is headed 'Clean Ship,' and it includes all the items of cleaning mentioned above.

The wise man, in drawing up his Excused List, starts off by showing no hands excused any 'Clean Ship' item at all. Then he reviews each case separately, and only when the claim to be excused is proved beyond doubt does he allow the claimant to escape out of the 'Clean Ship' rectangle.

The more hands to scrub the deck and clean the ship, the better for cleanliness and for contentment—let anyone bluff his way out and the loss in work will be far greater than the loss of one man's effort.

The Excused List must be easy to enter and to understand; the following are the necessary specifications:

(i) List of parties shown in alphabetical order both sides of the list.

(ii) 'Yes' and 'No' are muddling expressions and should not be used. 'Att.' and 'Ex.' are preferable.

(iii) The list should be produced as a large-scale drawing and framed and mounted at the correct height of eye in some frequented space or gangway.

(iv) Properly illuminated.

(v) Kept corrected up to date.

No time or trouble given to the Excused List can be wasted.

(*b*) *Division of Labour.*—The division of the ship for cleaning purposes among the parts of ship must be planned, and will require adjustment to avoid 'holidays' or overlap—an example is given in Part II.

(*c*) *Cleaning Gear.*—The distribution of cleaning gear needs careful checking, as does wastefulness.

(*d*) *Spoiling Good Work.*—If thoughtless and careless men are allowed to spoil the good work of others, even the best will lose heart. Disciplinary measures are necessary, and the policy has to be made clear to all hands (see 'Ten Commandments,' No. 2).

2. *Personal Interest.* (*a*) *Going Round the Ship.*—The Commander should unfailingly go round the ship by boat every day in harbour, before Divisions, taking with him, as a committee of taste, the Mate of the Upper Deck, Officers of Seamen Divisions, the Boatswain, the Chief Boatswain's Mate and the Captain of the Side. One advantage of a fair-sized party of officers and petty officers going round is that it makes their mission quite unmistakable to those inboard, and stimulates Captains of Tops and others.

At first it is easy enough to pick up faults, but after a time persistence meets its reward, and it will require the concentrated efforts of the whole committee to find a single rope yarn out of place.

(*b*) *Going Round the Deck.*—During Divisions the Commander should walk round the upper deck, the Captains of Tops standing rounds, and similarly at Evening Quarters, to ensure that the deck is left properly squared off after 'Clean Ship' and at the end of the day's work. The bridges should be reported cleared up and correct at Evening Quarters, and they should be visited occasionally during the Commander's rounds.

(*c*) *Officers Away in Boats.*—When away from the ship in boats, officers, and particularly the Midshipmen, have a good opportunity for looking her over critically and calling attention to faults. A seaman's eye for a smart ship is only developed by constant practice, and it adds greatly to the interest of a boat passage if an eye is cast over other ships.

(*d*) *A Smart Ship.*—Points that need continual attention in harbour, by those on deck, include:

Boats and Boat Gear.

Boat davits: Guys and fore and afters taut.
Falls rounded up.
Life-lines taut.
Slips stopped up to davits.

Boats square at davits.

Booms square: Boom guys and life-lines taut.

                    Boat-ropes hauled up clear of water when not in use.

                    Jacob's ladders not coiled up when no boat at boom.

Boat-ropes on accommodation ladders hauled up when not in use.

Duty boats: Appearance and cleanliness of boats and crews.

                    Boat-hook drill.

                    Handling and conduct of boats.

Derricks.

Main derrick purchase and topping lift taut.

Small derricks whips and guys taut.

Boats at small derricks at same level.

Funnels.

Funnel guys taut.

No smoke from funnels.

Quarterdeck.

General tidiness of quarterdeck.

Look out for dirty boots.

Dress and general bearing of dutymen on watch

Accommodation ladders and stays kept weeded.

Signals.

Signals promptly answered.

Halyards taut.

Ensign, Jack and Flag close up and clear.

Yards and gaff square.

Miscellaneous.

Awnings hauled out.

Guardrails taut.

Guns, searchlights and rangefinders square.

If covered, the lanyards taut with the ends tucked away.

No ropes' ends, dead ends or stray yarns lying over the side, from guardrails or awnings.

Ropes coiled down; ends whipped or pointed.

XXVI.   A FEW WORDS ON PAINT

(*a*) *Putting on Paint.*—There are three essentials for good paintwork:

(i)   *A Good Surface.*—This is achieved by washing the old paint and smoothing it off with pumice-stone or glass-paper. If any rust is showing, scrape it away and apply red lead (three coats, each to be smoothed off) before the paint goes on. If the surface is really smooth and clean, the paint will have twice the ordinary life.

(ii)   *The Right Paint.*—Well mixed with the right ingredients, strained, and fairly thin; the thicker the paint, the more any roughness underneath will show up. Paint-wash is a cheap and effective way of renewing paintwork, once the proper foundation is there.

(iii) *A Proper Finish.*—The correct way of applying paint is with horizontal strokes, finishing off with upward strokes. All strokes must be firm and the brush not overloaded. Painting is an art acquired with practice, and it is waste of paint to put a brush in inexperienced hands.

(*b*)   *Care of Paintwork.*—Paint is an expensive item on the Commander's Store Account, and once having been properly applied it has to be cared for.

(i)   *Cleaning Paintwork.*—After rain, returning from sea or doing anything which dirties the paint, wash it as soon as possible with fresh water, no soap being used on any enamel. For the latter use cold water and a chamois leather. Powdered brick may be used on the cloth to remove stains, but caustic soda should not be used.

(ii)   *Renewing Paint.*—It is not economy to delay renewing paint for too long, as the surface will be lost.

(*c*)   *The Side Party.*—The side party needs strong reinforcement on return to harbour; not only will they have the cable to paint, but the side must be washed and rust marks cleaned off.

(*d*)   *Scrubbing Decks.*—Care is needed when scrubbing decks to keep water from splashing on to paintwork and over the side—any paintwork affected should be washed with fresh water immediately.

(*e*)   *Masts and Funnels.*—Nothing smartens up a ship more than clean and shining masts, tops and funnels.

After being at sea and at regular intervals in harbour you should clean down. Paint-wash is suitable for funnels.

'. . . My Deck ! ! ! . . .'

MY GOODNESS
MY PAINT !

(*f*) *My Goodness!*—If a ship has some very special lobby or surface which it is decided to enamel, with a finish so perfect as to take away the cat's breath when he sees his whiskers, then the work must be done by the most expert painter. In his hands the following procedure gives the desired result:

(i) Rub down hard with pumice-stone and water.

(ii) Two thin coats of flattening, specially strained through fine copper wire gauze.

(iii) Rub down each coat of flattening with glass-paper and a special rub on the second coat.

(iv) Flood the enamel on—work it about with cross strokes, finishing with the usual vertical strokes.

(v) Renew it before it deteriorates, as a light rub down of the surface with pumice-stone is all that will be needed before applying the new enamel. And the second coat will look even better than the first.

(*g*) '*Shove off forrard.*'—Why should it be necessary for a boat leaving the gangway to give the nicely painted side a good push with her boat-hooks every time, and so damage the paintwork right alongside the front doorstep? It is in fact unnecessary, and a well-handled boat with a good crew should lie at the gangway so that she can cast off and leave without any pushing at all, and without any word being spoken. The order to the engines to go ahead is sufficient to warn the crew to let go fore and aft, and away she goes without any of this 'Shove off forrard' business. Devastating work on the side is done by those who forget that when their boats are lying alongside in a tideway they need steering all the time.

(*h*) *Damaging Paintwork.*—Reference has been made under the 'Ten Commandments' to those who lean against and ill-treat paintwork—the product of other men's skilled and painstaking labour. The punishment of being put on duty as a sentry is effective.

XXVII. OVERALL SUITS—A POLICY

Some hard thinking and some clear thinking are badly needed on the vexed question of the most suitable working rig for the modern seaman—a technician at work in the elaborate machine that is now a man-of-war. In climates unsuitable for duck suits or for tropical rig, an overall suit is beyond question the most suitable article of clothing in a sailor's kit as a general working rig.

There are no fixed rules with regard to the wearing of overall suits by seamen; the orders on the subject in various ships tend to be framed on the principle of restricting as far as possible the wearing of the overall, and at all costs keeping it out of sight on deck, rather than of providing a constructive solution to the problem of a suitable working rig. The result is unsatisfactory, in that the few only are catered for, and these shun the upper deck.

There is a natural and understandable antipathy on the part of the executive officer of a smart ship to the overall suit—the garment of the garage hand. And this antipathy leads to restrictions being imposed on the wearing of these suits, restrictions which may be based more on tradition or prejudice than on reason.

What are the hard facts of the case?

(*a*) The overall suit is the recognised working rig of the engine room department and of all artisans. Their kit includes two overall suits. A seaman has only to have one.

(*b*) In the case of seamen, the executive department sets out to restrict the overall suit to the Torpedo Party and to certain Standing Parties who work between decks. This policy is not uniformly successful.

(*c*) Out of sight is out of mind, and so long as the overall suit does not appear on the upper deck all goes smoothly, but the adverse effect on the health of the hidden wearers is manifest.

(*d*) Seamen working on the upper deck in their parts of ship are not allowed to wear overall suits, though some of their individual tasks may be unsuited to a serge suit.

(*e*) Nothing looks worse in this world than a paint-spotted and grease-stained serge suit, silk or collar, flannel or jersey, and they don't stand much washing or cleaning.

(*f*) Damaging good clothes is expensive—the cost of an overall suit is one-fifth of that of a seaman's rig.

So what is to be done about it?

The following main lines of policy are suggested:

(i) *Seamen Working in Part of Ship.*—For many reasons, traditional and aesthetic, they must be in the dress of the day unless the ship is out of routine. Captains of Tops should have authority to send men away to pull on overall suits for any job likely to dirty their serge suits. This authority to be extended to Coxswains of Boats on the booms.

(ii) *Seamen Working in Standing Parties.*—For working between decks they may wear overall suits. For working on the upper deck as for part of ship (above).

Note.—To share the wear and tear, duties to be changed to give men equal time in part of ship and in standing parties during the commission.

(iii) *Working Parties* to wear overalls for purposes which would spoil serge suits.

(iv) *After Working Hours.*—No one in the ship to be allowed to keep on an overall once work is finished, unless he is actually on duty, or a watch-keeper and on watch. 'Off Overalls' to be piped and enforced strictly.

(v) *Breakfast and Dinner Hours.*—All men authorised to wear overall suits may wear them on the upper deck in the breakfast and dinner hours for smoking before work.

(vi) *Clean Overalls* to be put on every Monday; all seamen who wear overalls to be inspected before turning-to that day. The seamen concerned will be required to add a second overall to their kit.

The Future.—Wanted! a practical working rig for the modern seaman: it would solve most of our overall problems. The requirements of cooler climates seem to be some form of washable seaman's suit made of a similar but better material than the overall. It should be a better fit than the present overall, which always tears under the arms. The drawback in making it a two-piece suit is that the two pieces would soon be washed different colours. Such a rig would be more practically suited to the modern seaman's work than the present serge suit; it would be smarter and more seamanlike than an overall or a grubby serge suit, and it would be warmer than a duck suit.

If a seaman is given a tidy yet practical working rig, he will take more trouble to keep it clean, and to appear smart, than if he is given an overall which fits like a sack and cannot be made to look smart.

TRAINING

XXVIII. MIDSHIPMEN WORKING FOR A 'FIRST' IN SEAMANSHIP

A First Class.—Although every Midshipman cannot get a 'One' in seamanship, it is nevertheless a very proper ambition, and seeing that ours is a Sea Service and that before all else we must be seamen, there is a natural desire to be rated first class in the fundamental business of the profession; it is not always the best seamen, however, who come out on top in the examination.

Even if all cannot get firsts, there is a genuine satisfaction in having done one's best, whatever the result, and in order to produce the best possible answer a plan of campaign is necessary.

Defects of the Usual Plan.—The usual plan when working up for the examination is for Midshipmen to be excused all ship duties as far as possible in the last three months of their time, and to settle down to an intensive cram. There are three reasons against this:

   (i) To lose touch with the routine and the work of the ship in all her varied activities involves separation from atmosphere and experience essential to the purpose in view.

   (ii) Cramming in the last few months produces a candidate for examination who is a walking encyclopædia of book knowledge, as opposed to a practical seaman well grounded in his subject and able to give common-sense answers to common-sense questions.

  (iii) Cramming also results in physical and nervous strain, thus weakening the candidate, and proving a bad prelude to the proper stage management of his appearance before the Board.

A Better Plan.—Instead of cramming at the end, it is suggested that a better plan would be to regard the whole of the last year as the working-up period for the examination, gathering speed steadily whilst keeping touch with the ship, and thus getting a far better take-off at the fence than from a short, sharp rush.

The Examination.—The examination resolves itself into two very nearly equal parts:

1. Former service ⎫
   Construction ⎪
   Signals   ⎬   .   .   .   450 marks.
   Journal   ⎭
2. Examination by a Board   .   550 marks.

The Factor of Chance.—It is a commonplace to say that the result of an examination of this kind is largely a matter of luck, depending among other things on the disposition of the members of the Board, friendly or unfriendly, and on the standard of the other candidates before the same Board. Luck always plays its part in human affairs, but timely forethought and preparation can also have their influence. It becomes a question of analysing the examination and making a deliberate and planned approach. If, from now on, the sordid matter of marks seems to be rather highly stressed, it is only because the problem must be studied close up.

Loading the Dice.—For a first class it is necessary to obtain 850 marks out of 1000—that means, therefore, that one can only afford to drop a total of 150.

As shown above, the examination is divided into two distinct parts—one is completed prior to meeting the Board, and the second consists of an individual performance in front of the Board. The element of chance can be almost entirely eliminated from the former half. To consider this in detail:

Part I

Former Service.—A Midshipman who goes all out for his ship in work and play is likely to earn 90 per cent. = loss of 20 marks.

Construction Paper. ⎧ The syllabus is absolutely cut and dried
                      ⎪ and no surprises are possible. By sheer
V/S and W/T   ⎨ determination and application, the
Papers.   ⎪ average brain should master these to
                      ⎪ the extent of 80 per cent. = loss of marks
                      ⎩ about 30.

Signals, Practical.—A question of regular practice and conscientious attention to signal exercises. Should get full marks = little or no loss.

Journal.—Take trouble over it = little or no loss.

If a Midshipman, therefore, makes up his mind to a steady and determined effort in his last year, there is nothing to prevent him from arriving in front of the Board having lost only 50 marks in Part I, and still having 100 marks to spare towards a first.

Part II

The Board.—If this has been achieved in the first part, less than 82 per cent. will be required from the most critical and hazardous part of the examination. That is a position of distinct advantage from which to face the Board.

Working up for this will cause most anxiety and difficulty; with two exceptions of Rule of the Road, a matter of exact legal fact, and of a handful of mechanical and numerical data, seamanship is an inexact science. The majority of problems that have confronted seamen down the ages have been those to which their sea-sense has had to find a rough-and-ready answer, most often by methods of trial and error. A textbook such as 'Queries in Seamanship' is misleading, if the reader regards it as providing an alpha and omega of possible questions. The problem is not to find out the ten thousand and one likely questions to which the one and only answer must be known in advance. There are far fewer questions than that, but to most of them there are a great many possible and passable answers. What is needed is quiet and steady assimilation of the Seamanship Manual, the Station Bill and the organisation of the ship, added to watchfulness over all and everything appertaining to the art of a seaman in ships and boats. This will bring the candidate far better prepared to the Board than will an encyclopædic collection of parrot answers to a rigid catalogue of questions. The reaction to an unexpected question must not be, 'Why didn't I think of that one before?' It must be something like this: 'I give him credit for asking common-sense questions, and if I think quietly for half a minute I shall probably find a fairly good and common-sense answer to any question he may ask, even if I have not met it before.'

Stage Management.

Nothing must be left to chance when the time comes to face the Board.

Be smart in appearance.

Be cheerful.

Don't look pained by the question—or puzzled, or uncertain of your answer.

Don't let them see 'fear or sad distrust in your eye.'

Answer the question fully.

Never say 'I don't know'—that puts you wrong at once. Infer, politely, that you don't quite understand the question—that puts him wrong. And he may let slip the answer.

Speak up—many of your seniors are hard of hearing.

Don't look for a catch in a question—there isn't one.

The question is almost certain to be straightforward.

The Answer.

The Board has to decide who is—

Above the average . . .	First class.
Average	Second class.
Below the average . . .	Third class.

As a Midshipman enters his last year he should take a grip of the task in front of him, so that on the *day* he will possess something that the others haven't got, and that will put him

ABOVE THE AVERAGE.

XXIX. PASSED MEN

Developing Power of Command

Requirement of the Organisation.—The executive organisation has to provide opportunities for the promising younger seamen to practise and develop the power of command that is latent in them. If an Able Seaman who is passed for Leading Seaman spends the period of waiting to be rated in doing duties which never require him to take charge or give an order, it is not surprising if, when the time comes, he 'cannot say boo to a goose.'

Able Seamen passed for Leading Seamen.—The objective is to ensure that every Able Seaman passed for Leading Seaman has chances, both in his daily work and at his action station, to take charge of one or more men. It is not too easy to find them suitable employment for this purpose. One-man jobs, such as sweepers and messmen, are entirely unsuitable.

Upper Deck Duties.—Passed Able Seamen can be given the following duties:

(*a*) Leading Hand of the Watch.

(*b*) Second Coxswain of Power Boats.

(*c*) Charge of small Standing Parties having no Leading Hand.

(*d*) Second in charge of larger Standing Parties, *e.g.* Second Captain of Side, and in opposite watch to the rating in charge of the party.

Leading Hand of the Watch.—He carries out the same duties for seamen as the marine corporal of the gangway carries out for Royal Marines.

He musters and inspects and generally takes charge of the call-boys on watch. Helps to run the routine and does certain rounds.

Brings defaulters up before O.O.W., other than higher ratings or marines.

Acts as Second Quartermaster, taking charge of one side when boat traffic is heavy.

His duty as Leading Hand of the Watch is invaluable in bringing out the command qualities of passed men, and, incidentally, he removes a cause of irritation frequently arising from a seaman being ordered to take off his cap by a marine, when brought before the O.O.W. It should be noted that the 'Corporal of the Gangway' is usually a marine, and not a corporal, nowadays.

The performance of this duty also brings passed Torpedomen to the front, and to the general notice of the executive officers.

Second Coxswain of Power Boat.—The senior rating in the boat should be a passed man if possible. He can frequently take the wheel, and he acts for the coxswain in the latter's absence, when cleaning out and refitting.

Gunnery Duties.—The following gunnery duties should be allocated in preference to passed men:

- (*a*) Gun-layers of hand-worked guns (Captain of Gun).
- (*b*) Breech-workers of hand-worked guns (in charge of loading).
- (*c*) Supervising numbers in magazines and shell-rooms.
- (*d*) Section Leader in Landing Parties, if no Leading Seaman available.

Acting Non-substantive Ratings.—In forming training classes on board for higher acting non-substantive rating, first selection should be made from the passed men, in order to aid their mental development, and to improve their status on the Quarter Bill.

Rosters of Passed Men.—Up-to-date rosters of passed men should be kept prominently in the Commander's, Gunnery, Torpedo and Divisional Offices.

Conclusion.—Once a man is passed for Leading Seaman, the critical time of waiting on the roster commences, and the development of powers of command of passed men during this period is without question one of the most serious responsibilities which the executive organisation has to shoulder. The consequences to the Service are far-reaching.

MISCELLANEOUS IDEAS

XXX. THE SPIRIT OF EVOLUTIONS

'If in reefing topsails you happen to be a minute later than another ship, never mind it, so long as your sails are well reefed and fit to stand blowing weather.

'Many a sail is split by bad reefing, and many a good sailor has lost his life by that foolish hurry which has done incredible harm in the Navy.'—COCHRANE.

1. *All Fair in Love and War.*—Let us hope that the bad old days of wooden bower anchors, and of torpedo nets held up by a split yarn, are gone for good; but as Evolutions tend to produce over-keenness, the Commanders in a squadron need a gentleman's agreement that, while doing all that is possible to pass to windward of the rest, they will permit no infringement of the principles of good seamanship.

2. *Single Ship Drills.*—In working up for the occasion when General Drill will be ordered, a ship first of all needs to drill by herself. The spirit of competition being the essence of Evolutions, it should be introduced into single ship drills, if the hands are to learn to work on their toes. Parts of ship, pairs of boats, port and starboard watches can all be made to compete against each other. Once the hands have learnt their stations, a drill day is dull without the zest of a race to liven things up.

3. *Passing Orders at Drill.*—To exercise instant control of the hands by the quick passage of clear orders, a microphone with the necessary loud-speakers on the upper deck is essential. Boatswain's Mates patrol near the speakers to repeat with the pipe any order missed through noise or other causes. In older ships where the equipment is not provided, it may have to be acquired by other means.

4. *Station Bill.*—No attempt is made in this book to supply a station bill. If the ship has not already got one, it will be necessary to ferret around the upper deck, planning out the drills and the division of hands, probably using the station bill of some other ship as a guide.

5. *Part of Watch Organisation.*—The fundamental reason for doing practice drills is to increase efficiency for the day when they may be required for service. When that time comes, there may be only a watch or part of watch on board, and this seems a convincing reason for basing the station bill on a part of watch, as opposed to a part of ship organisation.

6. *Picking up Lifebuoys at Sea.*—The trouble taken in working out every detail of this evolution in advance, with the Midshipmen and coxswains of sea-boats, is well repaid. It is a satisfactory drill in which to do well, possessing as it does the direct and obvious purpose of saving a life. Therein it differs from some other drills—for instance, it is not easy to see what another ship could want with all your wire hawsers.

To facilitate removing the calcium lights quickly after recovering the buoy, fit small brass lugs to the containers. Otherwise the sternsheets and stroke oars get choked by fumes.

When exercising sea-boats, all the precautions necessary for bad weather should be taken as a matter of course, in order to avoid being caught napping, when a boat has to be used in circumstances which involve danger to the crew and the boat.

7. *The Dog-Watch Evolution.*—At the end of a good day's work the leisure of the dog watches has been well earned. A Dog-Watch Evolution, such as lowering sea-boats at Evening Quarters, has all the demerit of tending to become a set piece, in place of the surprise evolution which it should be, and it needlessly prolongs the working day and encroaches on the dog watches.

8. *Tow Forward.*—It is generally agreed that an 'ocean' tow, which includes towing disabled ships out of action, as when *Indomitable* brought *Lion* home from the Dogger Bank, should and would be made with a single tow-line.

'Tow Forward' in the Service is frequently complicated as a drill, by adherence to the idea that it is desirable to provide, and to use simultaneously, two sets of hawsers, presumably with the intention of occupying all hands.

There is as little room for two sets of hawsers on the average forecastle as there is for two projectiles in one gun.

It is suggested that this evolution should be planned and practised strictly along the lines that are likely to arise through storm and battle, or from other misfortunes at sea.

9. *The Heaving Line.*—There is scarcely a seamanlike evolution in which the modest heaving line is not required to play its decisive part. An Inter-Part Line Throwing Competition, held periodically, helps to focus attention on this sometimes neglected art, and results in an improvement in throwing

'. . . THE MODEST HEAVING LINE . . .'

which is well-nigh incredible. Practice helps to make perfect, and the competition also serves to put the seamen on their mettle when champion line-shooters appear unexpectedly, as they do, from among the non-executive ranks. Those who can throw ten fathoms and more are to be found among all departments of the ship's company.

XXXI. BIG SHIPS AND SMALL SHIPS

There are many ways in which a big ship can help to make life easier for a small ship in her company.

The modern destroyers are self-contained units and there is little that a big ship can do for their internal comfort. But, apart from that, there are many ways of helping not only destroyers, but other small ships, and not forgetting the fleet auxiliaries. Here are some of them:

1. *Boat Assistance.*—Especially when trips are long or in bad weather. A copy of the boat routine and a special flag for calling routine boats alongside can be useful for this purpose.

Older destroyers need more boat help than the later ones, who are much better equipped in this respect.

2. *Shipwrights.*—The services of a shipwright or joiner are always invaluable when they can be spared.

3. *Workshops.*—The use of the big ship's workshop and particularly the welding plant for small repairs.

4. *Bread.*—When shore bread is not procurable.

5. *Entertainments.*—Any and every opportunity for seeing cinema and other shows are greatly appreciated and, in fact, any evening entertainment for the men is welcome. And a boat to fetch and return them.

6. *Recreation.*—Assistance with all forms of recreation and facilities for boxers, bayonet fighters and other warriors.

7. *Long Baths and Ice.*—No connection between these two, but both are very much appreciated by older destroyers and very small ships.

8. *Canteen Managers and Messmen.*—Big ship Canteen Managers and Messmen can be very useful to their small ship opposite numbers if liaison is encouraged.

9. *Small Ships affiliated to a Big Ship.*—These are the big ship's special concern, and in addition to the above a considered plan for the requisition of central stores, slops and pay is required. In other words, the Store and Victualling Officer of the affiliated ship should meet the Accountant Officer of the big ship early-on and get a working agreement.

The names of affiliated ships should be shown on a board in a prominent place, so that there can be no excuse for anyone in the big ship not knowing which are her particular small ships. A boy was overheard saying to another, while they were looking at the 'Affiliated Ship Board': 'Isn't that something to do with illegitimate children?'

'. . . ILLEGITIMATE CHILDREN . . .'

Make sure that yours have good reason to know who their 'Father' is!

10. *Close Liaison.*—A close liaison should be set up between the officers at the beginning of the affiliation or proximity.

There is often a hesitation on the part of small ship officers to go aboard big ships without invitation.

Very few big ship officers drop in on a small ship; the more we see of each other the better.

The above comprise yet another 'Ten Commandments,' and if a big ship could live up to these her name would be honoured among small ships. There must be many more ways in which one can help, and a small ship is quick to appreciate every consideration shown for her.

XXXII. MODERN HIGH-SPEED SERVICE BOATS

The advent of the high-speed motor boat in the Service has opened a new chapter of seamanship, and with it have come new problems for the Executive Officer, his Midshipmen, his coxswains, and his organisation.

These modern boats ride over the waves when they are fully planing, as opposed to their predecessors' ploughing through the seas, and their seaworthiness and general riding comfort have to be experienced to be believed, even under the worst possible conditions of wind and sea, and in the smallest type of planing boat.

Hoisting In and Out.—The hoisting weight of the modern 45-foot high-speed picket boat is about one-third of the weight of the steam picket boat that it replaces. This brings it within the weight of aircraft, and thus the cranes supplied for the latter are adequate for boat-hoisting, and the main derrick, with its cumbersome and elaborate rigging and its heavy demand on man's time, can be dispensed with.

Before hoisting, it is most important to see that the bilges are clear, as bilge water can form a large percentage of the total weight and cause inconvenience whilst hoisting.

Hints on Handling High-Speed Boats. (a) Effect of Light Draught.—Provided that it is borne in mind that the high-speed boat draws very little water compared with the normal round-bilged type of boat, it may be said that at low speeds the handling of these craft is much the same. The effect of the light draught is, however, to give a poor lateral grip in the water, so that a strong wind is likely to cause leeway and make turning at low speed difficult in one direction. Though fairly satisfactory in this respect, it must be said that directional control is not very good once the propeller has stopped turning ahead, and it is advisable for this reason that the propeller should be kept turning ahead until the last possible moment, so as to retain full rudder control. This type of boat loses its way very rapidly, and the boat can readily be brought to a standstill by means of a touch astern.

(b) Coxswain-Control.—In the case of the modern high-speed boat, coxswain-control will nearly always be adopted. The coxswain stands or sits at the wheel in the ordinary way, but, instead of ringing gongs to the engine room or working an

engine-room telegraph, he will move the reverse lever forwards or backwards as the case may be. The throttle, which controls the engine revolutions, will always be to his hand, but in manœuvring, the throttle should, as far as possible, be set to predetermined low revolutions of the engine, and left there except in case of emergency. The necessary operations to control the boat will then be confined simply to the use of a steering wheel and reverse lever, which would present no more difficulty than would be the case if there were a wheel and engine-room telegraph.

(*c*) *Going Alongside.*—There is, of course, a knack in getting the revolutions and the method of approach to a ladder or landing stage just right, but it is not greatly different from the knack which is necessary for bringing a steamboat alongside a ladder in a smart and seamanlike manner. It will always be found that there is a tendency for the stern of the boat to kick-off, either one way or the other, under the influence of the propeller turning astern; if, for instance, when going alongside a starboard ladder, it will be necessary to be prepared for this, by approaching the ladder at a fairly large angle and at the right moment putting the helm over, so that the stern is swinging towards the ladder when the propeller is reversed.

The above remarks apply to single-screw boats, but in the case of twin-screw boats manœuvring is much simpler, especially if the propellers are handed turning outwards for ahead. This factor is not, however, of so much importance in the case of small high-speed boats, as, owing to the high revolutions of the engines, the propellers are consequently small, and therefore cause little throw-off or torque effect.

(*d*) *Use of Throttle.*—In getting under way, it is essential to use the throttle gently in accelerating. The engines in these fast boats are of relatively high power, and damage can be done by rough use of the throttle. This precaution should also apply to throttling down the engines as well as to opening out. It is a bad practice, and almost equally damaging to an engine, to throttle down very rapidly, though this is not often realised. All movements of the throttle should be smooth and sympathetic to the engines. No boat should ever have to run with the throttle wide open except in emergency, or if special orders are given to this effect. It will always pay to run an engine at 300 or 400 revolutions less than the maximum permissible, and more than this if possible. In these planing boats it is, however, necessary not to try to run too slow except when approaching; with the boat only half-planing it is neither efficient as a planing boat nor yet as a displacement boat. Experience will indicate the correct speed to suit the conditions prevailing.

(*e*) *Running in Heavy Weather.*—When running before a heavy sea, it may be necessary in very bad conditions to ease down, owing to the possibility of 'broaching to.' In a fast boat with broad, flat sections aft, care must always be exercised when running before a sea, though 'hard chine' boats are better in this respect than a round-bilged boat of the fast type.

(*f*) *Short Seas.*—In heading into short seas, it may happen that, due to the speed of the boat and the short length between each crest, a more or less violent pounding is set up. When this becomes uncomfortable to the passengers it may be taken for granted that the boat itself is also being unfairly stressed; it is advisable to ease up a bit, or else to alter the course so as to take the waves as they come at an angle to the bow, on one side or the other.

(*g*) *Protection from Spray.*—A relatively small boat travelling over the surface of the water in bad weather, at speeds between twenty-five and thirty knots, must obviously be liable, in certain circumstances, to become splashed with spray from the bow wave, and it is necessary to afford proper protection to the coxswain and passengers.

Even in the worst conditions, however, it is quite possible to handle a well-designed boat so that very little, if any, spray comes aboard to an uncomfortable extent.

(*h*) *Watching the Wave Formations.*—It is difficult to lay down hard-and-fast rules for the handling of high-speed boats in all weathers because, like most other arts, close and intelligent observation is necessary, combined with the confidence gained by experience.

The approaching wave formations should be carefully watched, as the general riding comfort of the boat can be much affected by intelligent handling in driving the hull over the successive wave formations.

(*i*) *Turning.*—Care should be exercised in turning, as a rapid swing of the stern will undoubtedly tend to smother any occupants sitting aft in the boat with spray, much to their annoyance and discomfort.

(*j*) *Towing.*—Towing is quite practicable with the modern high-speed boat, but as the boats to be towed will mainly be of the more normal round-bottom form, it must be obvious that speeds in excess of six or seven knots are neither desirable nor practicable.

'. . . Old and New Navy . . .'

The propeller is designed for normal operation at planing speeds round twenty knots. Its proportions cannot, therefore, be expected to be correct for a towing speed of seven knots, which is below planing speed.

The tendency in towing will be for some excessive torque to be set up in the clutch and reverse gearbox if attempts are made to regulate engines at or near full throttle. It will be found that quite a small throttle opening will suffice for towing almost any load at reasonable speeds; it is important in the interests of the transmission gear that excessive speed while towing is not attempted.

With the above reservations, it will be found that these boats tow quite satisfactorily, and that their handling calls for no special technique.

Selecting Coxswains. (*a*) *Required Mentality.*—A slightly different mentality must be developed for the coxswains of high-speed boats, from that required to run the slower boats. In the latter the coxswain handled the steering, while an engineer handled the machinery.

The modern fast boat is usually controlled by one man, the coxswain, who, besides having charge of the steering gear, has also an engine throttle and reverse gear lever to hand, as well as the engine instruments to watch.

It is found at first that the necessity for thinking of three controls at once may give rise to confusion, but, like other controlling arrangements, once a certain amount of practice has been obtained, the necessary movements become practically automatic.

(*b*) *Different Types of Coxswains.*—Though in many ways simpler, the instruction in the driving and handling of these boats can be likened to learning to fly an aeroplane. Some individuals pick it up relatively quickly and soon become quite at home in all circumstances, while others are never really happy and are always more or less of a menace to the boat, and possibly also to its occupants. After a week, the coxswain selected should have mastered the job sufficiently to display, in all but the most trying circumstances, reasonable confidence and efficiency. If, however, he continues after this time to prove himself inept, it will save all concerned, and the boat in particular, if he is replaced by another man. Experience has proved that it is not necessarily a very young man who makes the best coxswain of these boats. In several cases a man approaching pension has proved to be suitable. The man to beware of is a man who 'knows all about it,' and who can be taught nothing by anybody. Though it is probably true that this applies to most walks of life, it is very much better to have the man who does not profess to have profound knowledge, but who, nevertheless, is painstaking and reliable and will ask if in doubt.

(*c*) *Mechanical Sense.*—The coxswain need not be a mechanic, but it is desirable that he should have at least the same degree of knowledge and sympathy for engines as is possessed by the good car owner and driver. He is likely to avoid, in these circumstances, violent use of the throttle or reverse lever, and the committing of such elementary mistakes as opening the throttle partially, or wide open, without the engine being clutched up to the propellers. Unfortunately, in the initial stages, this type of mistake is not so uncommon as might be imagined.

Notes on Maintenance. (*a*) *Preserving the Timber.*—The timber of which these boats are constructed is usually mahogany, which cannot be left bare owing to the effect of weather and damp, which will strain it and eventually cause rot. Unlike the scrubbed oak which is a feature of so many service boats, the mahogany must be left well coated with either paint or varnish, as the case may be.

(*b*) *Painting.*—Paint is relatively very heavy, and it is desirable that the application of coat upon coat should be avoided, by rubbing down well before application and periodical burning-off, say once a year. This routine will ensure superior appearance and finish.

(*c*) *Bilge Pumps.*—As weight plays such an important part in successful operation at speed, it is most desirable to see that the bilge ejection apparatus, either hand-operated or automatic, is kept in good condition and used at frequent intervals.

(*d*) *Before Full Calibre Firing.*—It is necessary to remove the glass cabin windows, which are usually designed with a view to simplicity of removal, complete with frames.

(*e*) *Engine Trouble.*—As the coxswain of a high-speed boat is handling the engine as well as the boat, it is essential that he should have sufficient knowledge to recognise the indications of possible engine trouble.

When a boat is running on passage, unusual sounds or behaviour of the engine must be closely investigated at once. A few of the more obvious troubles which may be experienced, together with the immediate action advisable, should form the subject of careful instructions to the coxswains.

(*f*) *Removal of Engine.*—Once an engine is run-in, and provided it is not allowed to go short of oil, it is unusual for anything to happen necessitating complete removal of the engine from the boat.

Should this, however, be necessary, the removal of the engine and the replacement by a spare engine of similar type, which is always carried in the parent ship, is a matter of about three-quarters of an hour's work. The defaulting engine can then be overhauled in the comparative luxury of the engineer's workshop, without the frantic haste occasioned by knowing that the boat is out of action until the repairs are completed.

XXXIII.　CEREMONIES

1. *Divisions.*—Hands should always fall in facing outboard at Divisions and Evening Quarters. Staring at paintwork is a deadly dull occupation, and viewed from outboard the appearance of the ship is enhanced by seeing the faces, rather than the backs, of those fallen in.

'Divisions' gives the chance of developing a certain amount of ceremony, and of exercising officers and petty officers in giving orders under ceremonial conditions.

When the Commander brings the Divisions from the stand-easy position to properly at ease by calling the ship's name, every man should brace up and grow a couple of inches.

2. *Piping.*—With very little attention, the standard of piping can be easily raised. Daily instruction for half an hour is desirable for the call-boys.

3. *Piping Meals.*—A massed pipe to meals on the upper deck by all the call-boys on watch, under the charge of the Boatswain's Mate, ensures that the call is initially piped correctly, and, furthermore, it gives the pipe to meals the deserved significance.

4. *Piping the Side.*—Very slovenly drill is often seen at the head of a gangway when receiving officers and in piping the side. A standard procedure should be worked out, and with the necessary fixed sequence of orders. All Quartermasters and others on watch must be given the required training. Constant pressure is needed until the desired degree of smartness is achieved at the 'front door.'

5. *Buglers and Bugling.*—A great ship should pass on her way, in and out of harbour, with a certain pomp and splendour and with a flourish of trumpets. For this purpose, a row of a dozen buglers against the skyline on the turrets at each end of the ship, seamen on 'B' Turret and Royal Marines on 'X' Turret, electrically controlled as one unit, and each group with their own bugle major, calls the very decided attention of other ships and onlookers.

There is no difficulty in getting volunteers, once they know the definite purpose for which the volunteers are wanted. Anyone with a note of music can be trained in the few simple calls required. Bugles are harder to come by, and one must beg, borrow or steal.

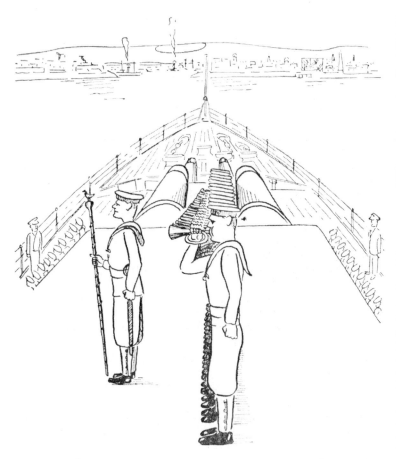

'. . . WITH A FLOURISH OF TRUMPETS . . .'

The seamen buglers wear belt and gaiters and the bugle majors wear sashes and hold a mace.

The seamen buglers look well when leading the march past at Admiral's Inspection; and also when drawn up in line near the gangway, they make an imposing addition to the reception committee for distinguished visitors to the ship.

6. *Entering or Leaving Harbour.*—The Commander needs to have the upper deck under his instantaneous control, when entering or leaving harbour, for a really smart effect to be obtained, and the loud-speaker equipment, previously referred to in this book in connection with evolutions, is invaluable in giving him this command.

7. *Ambassadors at large.*—Those who leave the ship on duty, whether as boats' crews or as patrols and orderlies, reveal their ship in many places, and to many people, who would otherwise never see or know anything of her at first-hand.

A clean boat is sometimes spoilt by men of indifferent appearance. Picked men, both as workers and on account of good physique, are the men to represent the ship in her boats.

Similarly, the men who land for patrol and other duties should be carefully selected, especially in foreign places.

8. *Brows.*—When a ship is lying alongside, it is important that the condition of her brows should be in keeping with her own smart appearance. Would a dirty accommodation ladder be accepted? Why, then, a dirty brow as a means of access to the selfsame spotless Quarterdeck?

Here are a few ways in which a ship's number one brow can be smartened up, and with very little trouble or expense:

(1) A good scrub over all.
(2) A coat of paint for the brow and its wheels.
(3) Planking over the treads, unless the steepness of ascent makes the treads necessary.
(4) Coconut matting, edged with white canvas, as a carpet.
(5) Detachable brass ends for brow rails.
(6) Canvas screens, edged with blue jean, for the length of the brow on either side.
(7) Ship's lifebuoys hung each side, from the centre, by wide brass hooks. The buoys to be enamelled white or dark blue, with the ship's name and crest in gold leaf.
(8) Suitable door-mats at both ends, with the ship's name worked in.

(9)   A line of indirect lighting under one rail and concealed by a strip of canvas. Naked bulbs are disfiguring and dazzling.

(10)   Teak rails beside the door-mats to ensure that no one avoids wiping his feet.

Once the necessary gear has been assembled, it will last for the best part of a commission and can be adapted to any brow. A smart ship must give the right impression on her front doorstep, as it will be the first impression gained by visitors, and probably the most lasting. When they see a clean brow, and incidentally a clean and tidy jetty, they will expect to see a clean ship. And they will be careful not to bring dirt on board.

9. *Payment.*—Pay being well and truly earned in working hours should be paid in working hours, and as a well-organised and swiftly conducted ceremony as opposed to a dinner-hour scramble.

10. '*Short Titles.*'—Subordinates should never be allowed to refer to senior officers by their telegraphic addresses, *e.g.* 'C.S. 10.' 'Please, sir, C.S. 7 is just coming on board' is typical of reports that are heard all too frequently nowadays.

Here is another instance. The Commander's messenger is questioned as follows:

Q.: Do you know what I mean by C.S. . . .?

A.: Yes, sir, the Admiral in the Cruisers.

Q.: What is his name?

A.: I have never heard of it, sir.

Surely we can find time, even in this age of hurry, to speak of 'Admiral Bowline,' or the Admiral of the Tenth Cruiser Squadron.

First Lieutenant.—'First Lieutenant' is a position which may be held by an officer of any rank from lieutenant-commander to gunner. If 'First Lieutenant-Commander' is used, then it would be only logical to speak of 'First Sub-Lieutenant' and 'First Gunner,' when a sub-lieutenant or gunner is filling the post of First Lieutenant. For similar reasons suspicion falls on 'Flag Lieutenant-Commander.' The 'Captain,' the 'First Lieutenant' and the 'Flag Lieutenant' are all offices and not ranks.

When I went as First Lieutenant of the *Excellent,* I found myself saddled with an office abbreviation of 'L.C. 1,' apparently standing for Lieutenant-Commander One; I even received letters starting 'Dear L.C. 1.' There had been First Lieutenants of the *Excellent* for over a hundred years, an office which, I am sure, my long line of predecessors had been as proud to hold as I was humbly glad to follow in their footsteps—but not as 'L.C. 1,' and I refused to accept any other title than 'First Lieutenant.'

There is a particular mentality which will never be satisfied until we have all become puppets of bureaucracy, with our identities concealed under office rubber stamps. That is not good enough for those born to inherit the tradition of the Roman centurion, and to say to men 'Go,' and they go.

If the dignity of a great traditional post such as 'Captain of Top' has not yet been undermined and weakened by a short title, it is only because he, lucky man, has no office work or paper work to deal with. The measure of the use and abuse of a short title, for one set in authority, is the measure of that individual's absorption, or otherwise, in his office desk.

XXXIV. ELECTRICS

(1) *Flood-lighting for Illuminating Ship.*—'Flood-lighting' is quickly supplanting 'outlining' for illumination of all kinds, but the Navy lags behind. Present-day illuminating circuits for ships are expensive and involve heavy labour in rigging and unrigging. In many ships outlining produces a caricature effect.

With flood-lighting, all of a ship's majesty and beauty can be revealed by light and shade effects, and the trouble involved in rigging is negligible. The cost is not great: one small ship contrived recently to be completely and most effectively flood-lit from her own resources. A big ship was able to achieve this partially.

The existing masthead illuminating circuits for destroyers produce a crazy effect, reminiscent of the look of a country circus, and they conceal rather than reveal the ship they are designed to illuminate.

(2) *Upper Deck Lighting.*—The parts of the upper deck where the hands gather together for talking, smoking, reading and playing cards are not usually provided with adequate or suitable lighting for these purposes. It is important both for health and recreation, and especially in warmer climates, that upper-deck smoking places under the awnings should have the character of well-lit reading rooms by night.

(3) *Ship's Telephone Service.*—The ship's telephone service is not always used to the full extent to which it might be. If fuller use were made, much running backwards and forwards by messengers could be avoided, and perhaps the number of messengers reduced.

A Ship's Telephone Directory, in a convenient form for popular use, is needed. The usual official list of numbers is crowded with every variety of little-used spaces in daily life, such as tiller compartments or hydraulic pump rooms.

For everyday use there are about fifty numbers that matter in a big ship, and an increased use of the telephone might result from these being issued in a small frame to hang by the telephone.

(4) *Electric Leads.*—For some unexplained reason the right is assumed, on behalf of temporary or portable electric leads, to do what no other form of rope or wire in a ship is allowed to do, namely to hang in bights.

This is said with no intention to reflect on the high standard of efficiency of the torpedo party; it is simply a fact. There seems to be no satisfactory explanation of why electric leads should not be stopped taut to a rail or jackstay, or why a run of electric wire should not conform to the line of the ship.

(5) *Indirect Lighting.*—Indirect lighting is the most effective illumination for a Quarterdeck, accommodation ladders, brows, lobbies, cup cases, and many other purposes, and is often easily fitted from ship resources. But the ordinary bulb light, naked and unashamed, continues to hold much of the field.

(6) *Mirrors.*—Mirrors combine subtly with schemes of indirect lighting to produce attractive effects in the show places of a ship.

RECREATION

XXXV.   TAKING THE CHAIR

The Executive Officer spends much of his time as Chairman of Committees. Wardroom Mess, Regatta and Football Committees are likely duties, and by King's Regulations he is *ex-officio* Chairman of the Canteen Committee.

The Canteen Committee is an important and influential body in a ship, and it was a surprise to be told by an officer who was Commander of one of our largest ships that he was seldom able to find time to attend the Canteen Committee, as so much of his time was occupied in receiving 'high-ups' at the gangway.

A Commander can very easily delegate his duty as Chairman of the Quarterdeck Reception Committee to a subordinate without offending anyone's dignity, but he certainly cannot delegate his position as Chairman of the Canteen Committee without risk of losing touch with essential things that closely concern him.

There is a small book entitled 'Taking the Chair,'[1] which is an invaluable guide and help in the duties of a chairman, and it is strongly recommended. Most of us are unaware that there is a definite legal procedure for the running of a committee, and an immense amount of time and trouble can be saved by a chairman who knows the ropes. Furthermore, it may happen that a ruling by the 'chair' is challenged by a sea lawyer, and it is unfortunate if the 'chair' is found to be wrong. It weakens the chairman's authority, and the committee has to start work all over again on the disputed item.

Captain Murray, in his chapter on the 'Agenda,' shows 'Any other business' as the last item. It has been found better, however, not to include that on the agenda of a Canteen Committee, as it results in every variety of spur-of-moment suggestions being sprung on the Committee, and the meetings being prolonged with interminable and usually fruitless discussions.

The Canteen Committee should meet regularly once a fortnight, and always at the same time and in the same place.

Smoking should be allowed.

---

[1] *Taking the Chair*, by Paymaster Captain H. P. W. G. Murray, D.S.O. Publisher, W. H. Barrell, Ltd. Price 1s.

The procedure adopted for preparing the agenda is given in Part II of this book.

Some irresponsible elements will appear on the first Committee of the commission—people with glib tongues: don't let them worry you—they are unlikely to be re-elected when their topmates know them better.

XXXVI. REGATTA—ORGANISING VICTORY

'There is only one way to win a Service pulling regatta, and that is for your crews to pull *harder* than the rest.'

The Importance of the Regatta.—The Pulling Regatta is the principal sporting event in the Fleet, and for a good reason. Eleven men only can represent their ship at football, and at cross-country running the largest team is thirty, but in a big-ship Regatta a team of nearly three hundred officers and men goes forth in the boats to do battle for their ship, and it is no wonder, therefore, that the Cock is the most highly prized of trophies; it is the reward of arduous training and of massed effort on a grand scale.

To win the Cock you need:

(*a*) The best organisation.

(*b*) The best ship spirit.

(*c*) The best training.

Some people grumble about the Regatta; but it does no good to waste time in grumbling; it is better to get down to it and go all out. If your luck is in, and even if you don't come out on top, but do well, you will hear no grumbling in your ship. There is nothing in this world to surpass the heartfelt satisfaction and delight of a ship's company when the Cock comes on board—it is a moment worth living for and worth working for.

Running the Regatta.—The man in charge has got a big task, and he needs all the support and the help he can get. It may or may not be the Commander, but the Regatta is a ship affair and a big one, and the Commander must be intimately associated. It is suggested that he should be Chairman of the Regatta Committee, and as such, at the head of a broad-based organisation of willing workers.

Regatta Committee:
Chairman: The Commander.
Members: All Racing Coxswains.
Any other officer or rating the Chairman co-opts.

The Committee should meet at least once a week during the training period. The minutes of each meeting to be published for general information.

Officers in Boats.—Every crew should have an officer who takes special interest in them, encouraging, coaching, and caring for them. There is no need for him to be an expert, but he should be prepared to give up his time.

Officers must go away with their boats from the beginning, but never to give orders—simply to watch and advise. And the first man to watch is the Coxswain: is he going to get a grip on them or not? If not, then you must seriously consider a change, and if a change is necessary it may be best to get the Captain to make it.

Racing Coxswains.—The essential requirement for a Racing Coxswain is that he should be a 'driver,' who is also well liked; the crews have to be driven down the course on the day of the race, and the easy-going, cup-of-tea type is no good at all. Nor is the wind-bag who has too much to say.

The driver is not necessarily a loud-voiced man. Many men of quiet but forceful personality will successfully dominate a crew and get the last ounce out of them.

The Racing Coxswains are an all-important body and must be treated as such. Forming them into the Regatta Committee makes them the best-informed men in the ship on Regatta matters. They are the *Corps d'Élite* of the organisation.

You cannot possibly give too much thought and too much care to choosing and training the Coxswains.

Regatta Oars.—Every man must have his own oar, and there should be a proper labelled stowage. It is necessary to build up a reserve of oars for some time prior to the Regatta. Individual oars are a psychological necessity, and economy results, as greater care is taken not to break them.

Racing Boats.—One flash boat may win races, but the Cock is not won that way. The Cock goes to the ship with the best and most level performance in all the races, and particularly in those in which she has two boats. All the same, nurse your racing boats carefully, as the effect on the spirit of the crews of your seeming to put a 'hoodoo' on the boats is profound.

Regatta Headquarters.—This is an important feature of the organisation, and the requirements are:

(1) A suitable place on the upper deck close to the position where Regatta boats are manned, and under cover.

(2) A large notice board with room for the practice timetable, record of training, local chart, and general information of all kinds.

(3) Microphone for the upper deck loud-speakers, used to call away the boats and for general information.

(4) A Midshipman in charge of the Regatta call-boys.

The Headquarters becomes the rallying point of the organisation, to which everyone turns for news. It may be possible to create a special smoking place for racing crews in the immediate vicinity.

How to Pull.—The small Service pamphlet, 'Boat Pulling, 1931,' is a good guide, and a suitable extract can be usefully made for officers and coxswains.

But don't let the theorists on 'style'—and they are many—blind you to the simple mechanics of the problem of moving a boat by oars; it is quite straightforward and is a matter of pure common sense. Transcending academic theories on style, what one needs above all is:

(*a*) The chance to win = organisation.
(*b*) The will to win = ship spirit.
(*c*) The fitness to win = training.

If these are achieved, your crews are likely to

'PULL HARDER THAN THE REST.'

H.M.S. "HOOD."

HOME FLEET REGATTA, 1935, AT SCAPA FLOW.

THE **CHUFFIOSOARUS.**

GEORGE

HOME FLEET REGATTA, 1935—RESULT.

1. **'HOOD'** 503   Points (Cock)
2. 'BARHAM' . . . 396½   „
3. 'RODNEY' . . . 360   „
4. 'VALIANT' . . . 310½   „
5. 'FURIOUS' . . . 284   „
6. 'NELSON' . . . 253   „
7. 'RENOWN' . . . 235   „
8. 'COURAGEOUS' . . 232   „

TROPHIES WON BY 'HOOD.'

THE COCK
BATTENBERG CUP
SEAMEN'S CUTTER CUP
COMMISSIONED OFFICERS' GIGS
SUBORDINATE OFFICERS' GIGS
WARRANT OFFICERS' GIGS
ALL COMERS CUP
THE PRINCE LOUIS CUP
(B.C.S. Warrant Officers' Gigs).
THE QUEENSTOWN CUP
(B.C.S. Subordinate Officers' Gigs).

PLACING OF 'HOOD'S' BOATS.

18 FIRST
6 SECOND
5 THIRD
} out of a total of 35 'Hood's' boats.

COMPARISON OF RECENT RESULTS.

Year.	COCK.	Percentage of Possible Points.	First Boats.	Boats Placed.
1935	'HOOD'	86	18	29
1934	'NELSON'	75	9	22
1933	'HOOD'	81	9	20

PRIZE MONEY WON BY 'HOOD'S' CREWS.

£70 : 10 : 0 out of a total of **£128 : 7 : 0.**

RESULT OF RACES.

FOR THE COCK.

	1	2	3	4	5	6	7	8	9	10	11	12	13	14	15	16	m.	s.
MONDAY, 5th JUNE.																	Time	
*Subordinate Officers' Gigs (Midshipman Gunner)	H	V	N	C	B	W	R	F									11	30
A.M. TUESDAY, 6th JUNE.																		
C.P.O.'s Gig (C.P.O. Yates)	H	N	W	C	B	V	F	R									12	35
R.M. Whalers (Corpl. Hayward)	H	R	F	V	W	C	B	N									12	38
*Stokers' Cutters (Ldg. Sto. Dobson and Sto. P.O. Vincent)	R	V	W	H	F	V	B	R	H	N	F	C	W	B	N	C	23	05
Seamen's Gigs (C.P.O. Damon and P.O. Edwards)	H	H	F	C	B	V	B	F	V	W	C	N	N	R	W	R	22	11
Seamen's Whalers (P.O. Dennis)	B	R	H	C	F	W	N	V									12	27
Young Seamen's Cutters (Ldg. Sea. Roberts)	H	B	R	V	F	C	W	N									11	27
*Commissioned Officers' Gigs (Lt.-Cdr. Dalrymple-Smith)	H	W	N	C	R	B	C	V	F	F							11	22
P.M.																		
*Seamen's Cutters (P.O. Plowman and Ldg. Sea. Douglas)	H	H	N	B	B	R	F	R	W	W	C	V	C	V	F	N	22	43
*Warrant Officers' Gigs (Warrant Engineer Bennett)	H	N	W	R	C	B	V										11	59
Stokers' Whalers (Ldg. Sto. Penny)	F	H	C	V	N	B	R	W									13	21
*R.M. Cutters (Corpl. Raven and Sergt. Christopher)	B	H	V	B	F	R	R	W	V	C	N	N	H	F	C	W	23	27
Artisans' Gigs (Shipwright Cole)	H	V	W	C	B	N	R	F									11	50
Miscellaneous Whalers (Ldg. Cook Godfrey and Ldg. Writer Wedick)	H	B	H	R	R	C	F	W	V	C	V	B	N	F	W	N	12	47
P.O.'s Cutters (P.O. Potter)	H	R	V	F	C	B	N	W									11	55
E.R.A.'s Gig (E.R.A. Fulcher)	F	B	H	V	N	R	C	W									12	49
Band Whalers (Musn. Sartain)	H	B	N	F	W	R	V	C									13	35
*Boys' Cutters (P.O. Davis and P.O. Bryan)	B	N	B	H	R	W	N	R	H	V	F	F	C	C	V	W	11	20
O.A.'s and E.A.'s Gigs (O.A. Underwood)	H	V	R	N	B	C	W	F									12	17
Signal and W/T Whalers (Ldg. Sig. Howell and Ldg. Tel. Bartlett)	H	F	B	R	H	F	C	V	C	R	B	V	W	N	N	W	12	31

*ALL COMERS.

1. 'Hood'	273	4. 'Courageous'	183	6. 'Furious'	156	
2. 'Rodney'	193	5. 'Nelson'	176	7. 'Valiant'	106	
3. 'Barham'	188½			8. 'Renown'	102½	

Cutters.	**Gigs.**	**Whalers.**
1st **'Hood'** (R.M.) (Cox: Major, R.M.)	1st **'Hood'** (Seamn. & Midshpn.) (Cox: Captain)	1st **'Hood'** (R.M. & Stokers) (Cox: Senior Engineer)
2nd 'Valiant'	2nd 'Furious'	2nd **'Hood'** (Accountant) (Cox: Paymaster Commander)
3rd **'Hood'** (Seamen) (Cox: Commander)	3rd **'Hood'** (Seamn. & Wardrm.) (Cox: Lieut.-Comdr. (T.))	3rd 'Courageous'

Time . . . 20 mins. 31 secs.

*Races for Challenge Cups.

FLEET RACES.

	1	2	3	4	5	6	7	8	9	10	11	12	13	m.	s.
Battenberg—Sub. Officers' Gigs	H	A	V	N	B	L	P	W	R	O				11	30
Rodman—Cutters	N	H	R	F	B	W	O	P	V	C	L	D	A	21	41
Drifters—Dinghy.	N	V	C	B	H	W	R							5	38

'Nelson'	N.	'Valiant'	V.		'Courageous'	C.	'Achilles'	A.
'Rodney'	R.	'Renown'	W.	**'HOOD' H.**	'Orion'	O.	'Leander'	L.
'Barham'	B.	'Furious'	F.		'Neptune'	P.	'Cairo'	D.

SIGNALS.

From . . Commander-in-Chief, Home Fleet to 'HOOD.'
'Please accept my sincere congratulations on your sweeping victory.'

———

From . . A.C.Q. to 'HOOD.'
'Well done, George. You thoroughly deserved it.'

———

From . . Admiral W. M. James to Captain Tower.
'A thousand congratulations to you and your crew on the great victory.'

———

From . . H.M.S. 'BARHAM' (Runner-up).
'Very heartiest congratulations from us all on your splendid win. Your crews were magnificent.'

———

From . . H.M.S. 'NELSON' (Holder of Cock).
'Hearty congratulations on your magnificent win.'

———

From . . H.M.S. 'CRUSADER' to H.M.S. 'HOOD.'
(*One Pompey Cock*)   (*Another larger one*)
'Please accept our heartiest congratulations.'

———

From . . H.M.S. 'ACHILLES' to H.M.S. 'HOOD.'
(*Cruiser Cock*)   (*Big Ship Cock*)
'From Bantam to Rooster—How's Yourself?'
Reply . . 'Cock-a-Doodle-Do.'

XXXVII.   OTHER SPORT IN SHIPS

Competitions.—Sport plays an ever-increasing part in the life of ships, and the competitive element enters strongly into the more important activities, such as football and cross-country running. The Regatta has already been mentioned, and these three are the principal competitions in which big ships are involved.

Pot-hunting.—It is easy to decry as pot-hunting the efforts of the enthusiastic to lead their ship to victory in sporting events, but those who say these things are often the ones who lack the spark of leadership, or the ability to organise, and the will to carry things through. It is in many cases a facile excuse for slackness or indifference. Opportunities to prove ability to lead are too few in times of peace for any to be neglected. Can there be any reasonable person who would sooner be in a dull and apathetic ship as far as sport goes, as compared with being in one which is keen and spirited? A good ship is one who is always 'there or thereabouts' in the achievement of anything to which she puts her hand.

There is no substitute for going all out for your ship whether in work or in play, unless, of course, you are prepared to toddle complacently towards your pension.

Inter-Part Games.—The proper basis for the organisation of games is the inter-part competition. It ensures the greatest number taking part and results in stronger teams to represent the ship. West Country ships are probably the only ones that can rise to inter-part rugger.

Every game needs its own committee of management, the more important having a representative for each division and the remainder a representative from each branch—seamen, marines, stokers, daymen and communications—with an officer in general charge of running each game.

Football and Running.—As with the Regatta, it is suggested that the Commander should act as chairman of a committee of officers and ratings who are keen to share the labours of organisation and encouragement in these two important sports.

Football is immensely popular, and good organisation not only provides games for large numbers, but also gives pleasure and interest to many others as spectators.

Running is a healthy exercise possessing the great advantages of needing no special pitch and of being unaffected by bad weather. It is not everyone's idea of fun, but it has an ever-increasing number of adherents.

King's Cup.—The Inter-Part Football Competition probably brings one hundred and fifty footballers into action, from whom an eleven is found to represent the ship in the King's Cup. Although only eleven men can be on the field, there is nothing to stop everyone else from being in support. 'Not Eleven, but Eleven Hundred' is a good motto for a big ship's football club.

Arbuthnot Trophy.—The Inter-Part Running Competition will bring as many as three hundred runners to the post in a big ship, from whom thirty are chosen for the Arbuthnot Trophy Race.

It is no wonder, therefore, that the Football Cup and the Bronze Man come second only to the Cock in popular estimation, and the three together make a great triumvirate.

Work and Play.—If a good fairy came to the Commander of a big ship and offered to make his dreams for the commission come true, what would he want?

I suggest he would ask to achieve:

> A well-disciplined ship.
> A clean ship.
> A contented ship.
> The Cock.
> The King's Cup, and
> The Bronze Man.

To make this possible she would need only one wave of her wand, as all these things are part of one and the same thing—a Good Ship!

XXXVIII. CINEMA

The cinema is a valuable asset to recreation on board ship, and in main fleets it is possible to get good films at reasonable prices by means of ships working co-operatively. The central organisation which has been created should make for steady improvement.

Films are, however, expensive items and they will probably remain so. The constant demand for better films has to be met, and although improved organisation may result in the price remaining steady, it is most unlikely to fall. If the Ship's Fund is to bear the whole of the burden, it is a heavy one, and leaves less money over than is required for other essential recreations.

Experience has shown that the men are ready and willing to contribute directly to the cinema, if the films are good enough, by paying for admission. A charge of twopence was made throughout a commission, and this worked successfully and greatly eased the strain on the Ship's Fund. Boys were charged one penny. A box office was established, with advance booking of tickets, to avoid men having to stand in a queue before the performance. More than half the cost of the films was directly contributed by the ship's company.

The comfort of the audience is an important consideration, and a great deal can be done from the ship's resources in the arrangement of seats, the shutting out of draughts, and efficient lighting. The satisfactory rigging of the auditorium is a concern of the duty officers.

Modern machines for talking films have the advantage of safety from fire, which enables the performance to be given between decks.

The Cinema Committee needs at least one moving spirit who is prepared to devote his leisure to the work, and there is full scope for imaginative direction by the officer in charge.

XXXIX. SHIP'S COMPANY WIRELESS

Essential requirements for the ship's company of a modern ship are:

(*a*) An efficient wireless receiving set, combined with a gramophone.

(*b*) Clear loud-speaker reception on all messdecks, enclosed messes, sick bay and in smoking places.

To satisfy these requirements a bold policy is called for at the outset. A new commission is well advised to obtain the best and latest equipment on the market, rather than to make do with what the old commission has left behind. A loan is readily obtained from the Sports Control Board for such a purpose as this.

Broadcast programmes, backed up by gramophone records, play a big part in life on board ship. Men are keenly interested in affairs of the day, and crucial pronouncements by statesmen unfailingly attract attentive crowds to the loud-speakers. The time of pipe-down has frequently to be deferred in response to a request to keep the wireless going, and the cause is as likely to be an important speech from London or Geneva as a 'big fight.'

There seems no reason why the wireless should be turned off for the Executive Officer's Night Rounds, but on the other hand an upper deck loud-speaker should have a local switch, in order to avoid interference with such work as hoisting cutters.

Having purchased a really good radiogram, it must be suitably housed where it can be properly cared for and operated. Its home should be proof against bad weather and gunfire, and adequately ventilated for the sake of the ratings who work the set. They are salaried by the Canteen Committee.

XL. SILENT RECREATION

Ship's Company Subscription Library.—The steady increase in the enjoyment of reading, both for interest and recreation, is only to be expected with the advance of education in the Service.

When opportunities for outdoor recreation fail, the book comes into its own, and the Subscription Library has proved its use beyond question, and has in fact become an essential adjunct to life on board a man-of-war. A wet day, with all recreation grounds unfit for play, and the issue of library books is doubled.

Two years' experience of running a Subscription Library in a big ship has shown that:

(*a*) The men are ready and willing to support, and to subscribe for the books they like.

(*b*) The creation of a library of about 2000 books and renewed by the periodical addition of at least 500 books a quarter is required.

(*c*) At a very small charge, the library can be entirely self-supporting.

Organisation of Subscription Library.—An officer is required in general charge; probably the Schoolmaster, with two volunteer librarians. The librarians should be men who are willing to devote much of their spare time to the library.

Finance.—A loan from the Canteen Committee enables the first purchase of 500 books to be made. The 3s. 6d. edition of books, which were first published at 7s. 6d., is a sound and serviceable investment, but due consideration must be given to books of higher price, and to the impression created by their presence. The average cost of books is £10 per hundred.

Rules of the Library:

(*a*) No initial deposit.

(*b*) One penny per book per week, paid when the book is taken out. No other subscription at all.

(*c*) A fine of one penny per book for each day that the book is retained over seven days.

(*d*) No borrowing of books except through the librarian.

(*e*) Lost books to be paid for at a proper valuation.

(*f*) Library to be open daily in the dinner hour, and for one hour after tea and supper.

(*g*) All books to be numbered and stamped.
(*h*) A register to be kept containing the title, number, the date issued, and the name of the borrower.
(*i*) List of overdue books to be compiled daily.
(*j*) Daily and weekly receipts checked, and entered in the ledger for audit.
(*k*) Suitable monthly remuneration to the librarians (*£2 per mensem* each).

Old books which have outlived their usefulness are always acceptable to smaller ships, hospitals or seamen's institutions.

Selection of Books.—Many suggestions come from those who use the library; after two years the proportion of different types in *Hood's* library was:

10 per cent, war books.
25 " " novels.
25 " " detective novels.
40 " " Wild West.

Average Weekly Results.—When the Subscription Library in a big ship is a going concern, the average weekly issue of books will be over one thousand and receipts about £5 per week.

The Ship's Library.—The Ship's Library, supplied by the Service to the ship on commissioning, contains some seven hundred books consisting in great part of the standard classical novels of the past and present, and thus forming a permanent standard library, whereas the Subscription Library will provide not less than five thousand books in the course of a two and a half years' commission of a big ship.

XLI.   MUTUAL AID

During a commission, cases of serious illness or of other grave misfortune at home will inevitably occur, calling for compassionate leave and consequent expense on travelling, which individuals are seldom in a position to afford.

In many ships some form of Mutual Aid Society has been successfully organised, conferring benefit not only on its members but also benefiting the whole ship, by relieving what would otherwise prove to be a heavy drain on the Ship's Fund. The latter is then left primarily available for recreational requirements—and a keen sporting ship can do with every penny.

With a capable and energetic secretary the membership of a big ship's Mutual Aid Society was maintained at over eight hundred throughout the commission, and this was in spite of many changes of personnel. The share-out at the end returned more than 80 per cent, of the money subscribed.

The following rules are suited to Home Fleet ships, and could be adapted to foreign service by adjusting the maximum sum for travelling:

Mutual Aid Society

Rules

1. *Objects of the Society and Grants.*—(*a*) To provide a sum of money, maximum £5, to cover the cost of travelling fares of any members who may be granted compassionate leave, exclusive of seasonal leave.

Should a member being on seasonal leave have to travel to some other place for compassionate reasons, he may refer his case to the Committee for consideration on completion of the leave period.

(*b*) Should a member die, the Committee be empowered to make a grant not exceeding £10 to his nominee.

(*c*) Should a member be invalided, the Committee be empowered to make him a grant not exceeding £5.

2. *Committee:*

President: Commander.

Hon. Treasurer: Paymaster Commander.

Five members: Elected by vote every six months. To be eligible for re-election.

Secretary: Must be a member of the Society.

3. *Subscriptions.*—The subscription shall be one shilling (1*s.*) per month. To be charged in the Ship's Ledger, in advance on the first pay-day in every month, and the total sum paid direct to the Honorary Treasurer.

Ratings now in the ship, when the Society is formed, to be allowed to join without entrance fee, provided they do so within one month of coming to the ship.

4. *Members Benefiting.*—Members who have received a grant are expected to continue their subscriptions for the rest of their service in the ship.

5. *Ceasing Membership:*

(*a*) *On Leaving Ship.*—If they have not benefited, to be refunded a proportion of subscriptions paid.

(*b*) *Withdrawal from the Society.*—Members withdrawing but remaining in the ship, to forfeit all claims to benefits or refund.

6. *Disposal of Funds on Ship Paying off.*—On paying off, the balance of the fund to be shared out among all members.

7. *Meetings.*—The Committee to assemble as requisite, and once monthly to decide on the rate payable for return of subscriptions to members leaving the ship.

Note.—Membership of the Mutual Aid Society will in no way disqualify ratings from applying to the Canteen Committee for financial assistance or possible assistance from the Royal Naval Benevolent Trust.

Any rating wishing to join the Society, or a member desiring information, should make application to a member of the Committee or the Secretary.

XLII.   SHIP'S COMPANY GUESTS

(*a*) *Pride of Ship.*—There is no surer way to increase a man's pride in his ship than for those who are near and dear to him to feel proud of her too. It is impossible to show too much courtesy and consideration in welcoming friends and relations on board on every occasion when it is possible for them to be invited.

(*b*) *Waiving Restrictions.*—All restrictions on brows, ladders and gangways such as are normally reserved for officers should be waived in favour of those who are the private guests of the officers and men, in order to facilitate to the utmost their opportunity of seeing the ship in privileged comfort.

(*c*) *Serving Tea.*—If it is possible to arrange for tea to be served on the upper deck in fine weather, or in some sheltered space at other times, so much the better. It is easily organised and for a small charge only.

(*d*) *Other People's Messes.*—It is reasonable to lay down that no one in the ship may show his private guests into any other mess than his own, unless by invitation or permission from the president of that mess. Everyone should be secure from the chance intrusion of strangers when in the seclusion of his own mess.

(*e*) *Cloakroom Arrangements.*—Adequate cloakroom arrangements are required which can be automatically put into effect on the regular days for private guests coming on board.

(*f*) *Ship's Boat Service.*—The ship's boats should be unreservedly at the disposal of guests, with definite routine trips, on make-and-mend days and on other special occasions of entertaining on board.

(*g*) *Promulgating Information.*—The fact that the guests of the ship's company have the freedom of the ship, except for confidential spaces, requires to be prominently stated on the Commander's Notice Boards, and repeated from time to time. An occasional reminder of this at the Executive Officers' weekly meetings is also timely in keeping the duty of welcoming ship's guests in the mind of those on watch.

Full information with regard to facilities for embarking guests, such as details of landing-places and boats, should also be posted in good time for the hosts to pass the word ashore.

(*h*) *The Ship's Company.*—A strictly legal definition of the term 'Ship's Company' embraces every person borne on her books. But in practice, if it is possible by the warmth of the welcome they are given to make all the families feel that they also belong, then the company of a big ship becomes multiplied from one thousand into several thousands. To have so great a community bound together both by family affection and by pride of ship must influence her fortunes decisively.

On foreign stations it will be the friends rather than the relations for whom the ship has to cater, but the principle of treating the private guest as a privileged person, in comparison to the ordinary ship's visitor, equally holds true.

PART II

Executive Organisation

The Executive Organisation laid down herein is to be conformed to by all Officers, Chief and Petty Officers and Ratings concerned.

Commander.

INDEX

(References are to *Sections*, not *pages*.)

H.M.S. . . . .

Distribution

Admiral's Staff.
Captain.
O.O.W.
Commander (N.).
Engineer Commander.
Paymaster Commander.
Surgeon Commander.
First Lieutenant.
Lieutenant-Commander (G.).
       ,,   ,,   (T.).
       ,,   ,,   (P. & R.T.).
       ,,   ,,   (U.D.).
Lieutenant (F.X.).
       ,,   (Top).
       ,,   (Q.D.).
Sub-Lieutenant.
Major R.M.
Captain R.M.
Comd. Gunner.
       ,,   ,,   (T.).
Senior Midshipman (for Midshipmen).
Master-at-Arms.
Chief Boatswain's Mate.
Captain of the Forecastle.
Captain of the Topmen.
Captain of the Quarterdeck.
Sergeant-Major.
President of C.P.O.'s Mess.
President of P.O.'s Mess.
Commander's Office (2).
Boys' Divisional Officer.
Lieutenant (E.).
Corrections: All corrections will be made by Commander's Office.

RUNNING A BIG SHIP

1. COMPLEMENT

The present authorised upper deck complement is:

Officers . . . .
Chief Petty Officers . . . . . .
Petty Officers . . . .
Leading Seamen . . . .
A.B. or Ord. . . . .
Boy 1st Class . . . .
Sailmaker . . . .

Total U.D.

Communications . . . .

Executive Total

Including in the foregoing:

Gunner's Mates . . . .
Director Layers . . . .
Gunlayers . . . .
Rangetakers . . . .
Seamen Gunners . . . .
G.L. Writer . . . .
Torpedo Gunner's Mate . . . . .
Leading Torpedomen . . . . . .
Seamen Torpedomen . . . . . .
T.L. Writer . . . .
P. & R.T.I. 2nd Class . . . . .
Buglers . . . .

Engineer Branch . . . .
Artisan Branch . . . .
Medical Branch . . . .
Accountant Branch . . . . . .
Regulating Branch . . . .
Royal Marines (plus Band) . . . . .

Authorised Total Complement

2. QUARTER BILL

Main Armament:

'A' Turret . . . . Manned by F.X.
'B' „ . . . . „ „ Top.
'X' „ . . . . „ „ R.M.
'Y' „ . . . . „ „ Q.D.

EXECUTIVE ORGANISATION

Secy. Armament:

	Port	Starboard
No. 1 Gun	F.X.	F.X.
No. 2 Gun	F.X.	R.M.
No. 3 Gun	Top.	Top.
No. 4 Gun	Top.	R.M.
No. 5 Gun	Q.D.	R.M.
No. 6 Gun	Q.D.	R.M.

H.A. Armament:

4-in. H.A. Guns	Manned by Q.D.
Port Mk. 'M' ⎱	
Pom-Pom ⎰	" " Top.
Starb. Mk. 'M' ⎱	
Pom-Pom ⎰	" " F.X.

Saluting Guns—Manned by Gunner's Party and 2 hands from each part of ship.

3. ORGANISATION BY DIVISIONS

Falling in at Divisions.

Division	Composed of		Fair Weather	Foul Weather
F.X.	F.X. men	Sun.	F.X. Starb.	Own Messdeck
		Wkdy.	Q.D. "	
Top	Topmen	Sun.	F.X. Port	Messdeck
		Wkdy.	Q.D. "	
Q.D.	Q.D. men		Q.D. Starb.	Messdeck
Torpedo	Torpedo Rtgs. &	Sun.	Q.D. Starb.	Messdeck
	E.A.'s.	Qtrs.	By Daylight Wksp.	outside Mess
Boys	All Boys	Sun.	Q.D. Port	Messdeck
		Wkdy.	Q.D. Starb.	
Air	All F.A.A. Personnel		As requisite	In Hangar
Communications	Tel. & Sig.	Sun.	Q.D. Port	Communication
	Ratings	Wkdy.	Q.D. "	Messdeck
R.M. Detachment	Royal Marines		Q.D. Port	Messdeck
Stokers—Red	Stoker Ratings, Red Watch		Port Battery	Messdeck
Stokers—White	Stoker Ratings, White Watch		Port Battery	Messdeck
Stokers—Blue	Stoker Ratings, Blue Watch		Starb. Battery	Messdeck
E.R. Artificers	E.R.A.'s & Mechanicians		Starb. Battery	Messdeck
Miscellaneous			Port Lobby	

Notes.

(1) When fallen in below, men are to be fallen in on their own Messdecks in file between mess tables, facing inboard.

(2) In wet weather Divisions may be piped to fall in in the

Batteries, when the positions will be similar to those at Evening Quarters in foul weather. (See below.)

Saturday Divisions.

(1) Divisions are to be fallen in facing outboard with all the Leading hands, Petty Officers and Chief Petty Officers forming a supernumerary rank in rear.

(2) Midshipmen will fall in in line with the front rank, one pace clear, on either flank. If there is only one, he will be on the side from which the Captain will approach.

(3) The supernumerary rank will be formed with the senior rating on that flank from which the Captain will approach.

(4) *On the order 'Off Caps' all Leading Seamen and below will take off their caps and the senior Chief or Petty Officer will salute and return to 'attention.'

*NOTE.—In normal circumstances the Captain does not wish caps to be taken off for his Sunday inspection, but will give a special order when he does require it.

Evening Quarters—Falling in Positions

The Quarterdeck will not be used. The following positions are used at sea and in harbour, all Divisions facing outboard.

STARBOARD SIDE	FAIR WEATHER	FOUL WEATHER
Fx'lemen	F.X. Starb. between Breakwaters	Starb. Batt. outside Galley
Torpedomen	F.X. Starb. abaft Breakwaters	Forward Embrasure
Topmen	Starb. Batt. Foremost half	Starb. Batt. Foremost half
Royal Marines	Starb. Batt. After half	Starb. Batt. After half
Air	As requisite	In Hangar

PORT SIDE	FAIR WEATHER	FOUL WEATHER
Boys	F.X. Port from Screen door For'd	Port Batt. outside Galley
Engine Room	Port Batt. Foremost half	Port Batt. Foremost half
Qtrdeckmen	Port " After half	Port " After half
Communications	Port Lobby	Port Lobby

Notes.

(*a*) In foul weather, the pipe will be 'Hands to Evening Quarters in the Batteries' and Divisions are, if necessary, to be fallen in four deep and moved into shelter from rain and wind.

(*b*) In fair weather Divisions are to be two deep.

(*c*) At sea, Commander on the Bridge receives reports of Officers of Divisions from Port side of Boat Deck, unless otherwise ordered. Mate of Upper Deck reports Upper Deck cleared up to Commander on Bridge.

(*d*) In absence of First Lieutenant, the Duty Lieutenant-Commander goes round the Messdecks during Evening Quarters and reports cleared up.

(*e*) When the warning pipe is passed that 'Evening Quarters will be in the Batteries,' Deck cloths on Upper Deck are not to be taken up, or if already up, they are to be put down.

4. AIR DIVISION

The Air Division includes all Officers and Men of the Royal Navy borne for duty with the ship's Air Arm.

(*a*) *Establishment:*

(i) *Operational:*

1 Pilot
1 Observer   .   .   . per 3-seater aircraft.
1 T.A.G.

1 Pilot
1 Observer   .   .   . per 2-seater aircraft.
or 1 T.A.G.

(ii) *Maintenance:*

2 R.A.F. Ratings
1 Able Seaman   .   . per aircraft.

N.C.O. Airmen, Armourers, etc., in addition, making the total maintenance personnel four per aircraft on an average.

(*b*) *Messing:*

All the Air Division, of and below equivalent rating of Leading Seaman, mess together.

N.C.O. Airmen of Sergeant's Rank live in Royal Marines Sergeants' Mess.

(*c*) *Routine:*

0615.   Turn out with Guard and Steerage.
0700.   Breakfast.
0750.   Air Division fall in.

Note.—Seamen of Air Division fall in with the hands at 0600 and clean Air part of ship.

Uniform:

R.N.	R.A.F.
No. 1.	Breeches and putties with best tunic.
No. 2.	Best tunic and slacks.
No. 3.	Tunic and slacks.
No. 6.	Best khaki tunic and slacks.
No. 7.	Khaki tunic and slacks and shorts.
	R.A.F. working rig in hot weather is shirt and shorts.

Note.

When dress for libertymen is No. 2, the R.A.F. should comply and wear their equivalent of best tunic and slacks.

5. BOYS

(1) *Boys' Division.*—Boys, including Boy Signalmen and Boy Telegraphists, form a separate division, known as the Boys' Division.

(2) *Instructors.*—For a division of over one hundred boys the following instructors are detailed:

1 Petty Officer:	In general charge of the division and for regulating duties.
1 Petty Officer:	For charge of messdecks, flats, bags, hammocks and kits.
4 Petty Officers:	As Boys' Instructors. Take turn as Duty Instructor. Assist with instruction of Boys' Training Classes.

(3) *Falling in and Mustering.*—At Divisions and Evening Quarters they fall in separately as a division. When the hands fall in for work, the boys are ordered to fall in when 'Out Pipes' is sounded. They fall in separately and abaft the remainder of the hands, and when mustered and correct, they are reported to the Commander by the Duty Instructor.

6. THE WATCH BILL

1. *Clear Lower Deck.*—Calls all men not actually on watch.

2. *Watch of the Hands.*—Calls all men in the watch of Seamen and Marines, as for 'Clear Lower Deck,' except duty boats' crews, double bottom party, cabin hands, buglers and writers.

3. *Watch or Both Watches.*—Calls all Seamen and Royal Marine ranks of the watch or watches named, except those excused in the Excused List.

4. *Part or Sub of the Watch.*—As for watch or both watches.

5. *Duty Hands.*—A Leading Hand and 2 hands from each part of the watch on deck. Primarily for use out of working hours.

The term 'For Exercise' is not used.

6. *General Policy with Regard to Employment of Hands.*— (*a*) 'Clear Lower Deck' will be reserved for 'Everybody Aft,' Payment, Open List and similar occasions. It is not intended to be used as a means of summoning hands for work or stations.

(*b*) 'Both Watches of the Hands' will be used when all available hands are required for work or stations. When hoisting boats in the dog watches, Part of the Watch of the Hands should be used; or Watch of the Hands, if the former is not sufficient to run up the boats that are being hoisted.

(*c*) If comparatively few hands are required unexpectedly during working hours, it is desirable to disturb the work of the ship and the Training Classes as little as possible. For this reason, 'Hands working on the Upper Deck' should be used wherever practicable. Similarly, '2 Hands from each Part and 2 Marines' should be piped in preference to Duty Hands in working hours.

7. Approximate Number of Hands in each of the foregoing:
    (*a*) Watch of Hands (159), (164).
    (*b*) Watch (76), (71).

8. *Remarks on Routine.*—Everyone is to be on deck at 'Hands Fall In' first thing, except watchkeepers. 'Both Watches of Hands' fall in at 0830 and 1315, when special parties will be mustered and fallen out. After weekday Divisions, 'Both Watches' will fall in. In the normal course, Captains of Tops are responsible for 'Clearing up Decks' at the end of working hours, without further orders.

7. DUTY PART OF WATCH OF HANDS

(1) *Numerical Lists.*—The Regulating Petty Officers of each Seamen Division, and the Royal Marines are to place in the Commander's Office by noon daily a numerical list of P.O.'s, Leading Seamen and Seamen who will fall in should the Duty Part of Watch of Hands be required:
    (*a*) In Working Hours.
    (*b*) After 1600.
    (*c*) After 2000.

A copy is also to be given by the Regulating Petty Officer to the Senior Rating of the Part of Ship in the Duty Part of Watch of Hands. This rating is also responsible that his own Watch Bill is up to date for mustering his Part of Ship.

The numerical lists are to represent the exact numbers available as per Excused List, Sick List, Special Leave, etc.

(2) *Commander's Office.*—Will compile a numerical list from the above for all Seamen Divisions and Royal Marines, and supply copies to:
    (1) O.O.W. (on a board).
    (2) Stand-by Officer.
    (3) Warrant Officer of day.
    (4) Duty Lieutenant-Commander.
    (5) Commander.
    (6) Seaman P.O. of the Duty Part of the Watch of Hands.

(3) *When Duty Part Falls In*—
    (*a*) Senior Rating in each Part of Ship musters his Part and reports to Senior P.O. of the Part of Watch of Hands, the number present.
    (*b*) Senior Petty Officer and N.C.O. report total numbers present to officer in charge.

(4) *On Completion of Work.*—Duty Part of Watch of Hands is *always* to fall in on completion of its work whether in or out of Working Hours and be mustered numerically as in paragraph (3) above.

(5) *Stokers.*—After Working Hours the duty part of Stokers will fall in with the Duty Part of the Watch, when it is required to hoist cutters.

(6) *Torpedomen.*—Except for boat hoisting the Torpedomen will not fall in with the Duty Part of the Watch. It is entirely their own responsibility that they are fallen in when boats are hoisted.

(7) *Warning the Part of the Watch and Stokers they will be Required.*—Fifteen minutes before cutters are hoisted, it should be piped that the Part of the Watch of Hands and Stokers will be required for hoisting boats in fifteen minutes' time. The following hands should then be fallen in:

(1) Duty Part of the Watch of Hands.
(2) Torpedomen of the Duty Part.
(3) Duty Part of Stokers.

8. HAWSERS AND CORDAGE: ALLOCATION

Forecastle

Description	Fathoms	Stowage
6½-in. Wire Hawser	150	F.X. abaft No. 1 B.W.
5-in. Mooring Pendant	56	F.X. Port abaft No. 1 B.W.
5-in. Cat Pendant	60	With Mooring Pendant
5-in. Cat Pendant	60	F.X. Port abreast screen
3-in. Mast Rope (Wire)	80	F.X. Starb. on screen
2¾-in. Cat Purchase (Starb.)	200	Boat Deck Starb. by Fore Funnel
2¾-in. Cat Purchase (Port)	200	F.X. Port abaft B Turret
4½-in. Picking up Rope	60	F.X. Port abaft No. 2 B.W.
6½-in. Wire Ganger	7	Cross Passage before W.R. Galley
8-in. Manilla (Destroyer's Oiling)	80	Starb. Battery outside Ship's Galley (Head Rope)

Topmen

3½-in. Wire Hawser (Starb.)	150	Boat Deck Starb. abaft Pom-Pom
3½-in. Wire Hawser (Port)	150	„ „ Port „ „
2½-in. Wire Hawser	150	„ „ Port abreast Stump Derrick
8-in. Manilla (Destroyer's Oiling)	80	Port Battery abreast P.4 (Fore Spring)
6-in. Manilla Hawser (Starb.)	113	Starb. Battery by Seaman's Heads
6-in. Manilla Hawser (Port)	113	Port Battery abreast Kedge

Quarterdeck

6¾-in. Wire Hawser	150	Boat Deck aft Starb.
4½-in. Wire Hawser	150	Boat Deck Port by Stream Anchor
1½-in. Fog Buoy Rope	300	Boat Deck Port Aft
5½-in. Wire Ganger	7	Cross Passage before W.R. Galley
8-in. Manilla (Destroyer's Oiling)	30	Port Battery abreast P.3 (After Spring)
8-in. Manilla (Destroyer's Oiling)	30	Outside W.R. Galley in Cross Passage (After Breast)
5-in. Grass Hawser	113	Boat Deck outside Coppersmith's Shop
5-in. Grass Hawser	113	Boat Deck below after link.

9. ALLOCATION OF BOATS, BOATS' FALLS, AWNINGS AND OTHER GEAR TO PARTS OF SHIP

	F.X.	Top	Q.D.
Boats	1st P.B.	Ship's M.B.	2nd P.B.
	Capt.'s M.B.	1st Launch	2nd Launch
	1st Cutter	2nd Cutter	4th Cutter
	3rd Cutter	Capt.'s Galley	Admiral's Galley
	Comdr.'s Gig	1st Whaler	2nd Whaler
		1st Skiff	2nd Skiff
Admiral's Barge	1	1	2

(Note.—M.B.'s have Cox and 2 A.B.'s with 1 additional A.B. in bad weather.)

Boats' Falls.—Will be rove by the part of ship whose cutter is hoisted at the davits.

Booms and	Starb. Lower	(1) Port Lower	(1) After Gangway
Boat-ropes	Boom	Boom	(2) Both Qtr. Booms
		(2) Fore Gangway	

Carley Floats			
Accommodation	1, 2	3, 4, 5	6, 7, 8
Ladders	None	Fore	Starb. After Q.D.

(Note.—Q.M.'s Staff cleans all   Port After R.M. ladders.)

Awnings	Q.D. Starb. Wing	Q.D. Port Wing	Q.D. Main
		Battery Awnings	Admiral's Deck
			Awnings (2)

Awning Curtains	None	Battery	Q.D.
Oil Naviga-tion Lights	Fore Steaming light	Bow lights	Main Steaming light
			Stern light

Note.

Signalmen are responsible for Not Under Control lights and Anchor lights.

10. ORGANISATION FOR CLEANING SHIP
(Upper Deck and above)

Forecastlemen.
(*a*) Forecastle.
(*b*) Outside Daylight Workshop. (Torpedomen before breakfast.)
(*c*) Both Embrasures (as far as P.3 and S.3).
(*d*) Admiral's Cabin Bridge.
(*e*) Admiral's Bridge.
(*f*) Compass Platform.
(*g*) Mainmast below Spotting Top.
(*h*) 2 P.V. Lockers.
(*i*) Sand Tank.
(*k*) Cable Lockers.

Topmen.

    (*a*) From P.3 and S.3, through full length of both batteries.

    (*b*) Boat Deck from after beading to fore end.

    (*c*) Foretopmast.

    (*d*) Fore Funnel.

Quarterdeckmen.

    (*a*) Boat Deck, from after beading to after end.

    (*b*) Mainmast above Boat Deck.

    (*c*) Main Derrick.

    (*d*) After Funnel.

    (*e*) After Superstructure.

Signal Department.

    (*a*) Captain's Bridge.

    (*b*) Flag Deck.

    (*c*) S.D.O.

    (*d*) Lower S.D.O. and Flat.

    (*e*) Signal Division Office.

Boats' Crews.

    Boats, Boats' Davits, Davit Guys with their Bottle Screws and Slips, Griping Spars, Jumping Ladders, Boats' Crutches by part of ship to which Boat belongs.

Navigation Party.

    (Clean all Navigating Positions and Gear), Chart Houses, Upper Conning Towers, Sounding Booms and Patent Log Brackets.

Torpedo Party.

    (*a*) Outside Daylight Workshop (before breakfast).

    (*b*) S/L Platforms, Nos. 1, 2 and 3.

    (*c*) T.C.P.

    (*d*) T.C.T.

    (*e*) Daylight Workshop.

    (*f*) After Range Tower.

    (*g*) Upper Plotting House.

    (*h*) Lower Plotting House.

    (*i*) L.T.O.'s Hut (on Forebridge).

    (*j*) Secondary Battery Room on Boat Deck.

5.5-in. *Gun Sweepers.*

    5.5-in. Guns manned by Seamen.

H.A. Sweepers (*under 'G.' Dept.*).

    4-in. Guns and wooden decks of Gun Platforms. H.A. Control Position.

    Inside of canvas screen round Gun Platforms.

Pom-Pom Sweepers (*under 'G.' Dept.*).

    Pom-Poms, and decks of Pom-Pom Supports.

Royal Marines.
Admiral's, Secretary's and W.R. Lobbies.
W.R. and G.R. Round-houses.

E.R. Department.
(*a*) Sirens.
(*b*) Funnel Guys.
(*c*) Disinfector Room.
(*d*) Coppersmith's Shop.

Note.
(i) *Turrets.*

Enamel outside by part of ship.
Top of Turret by Turret Sweepers.
Bright-work by Turret's Crew.

(ii) *Part of Ship Colours.*

Part of ship colours for painting on buckets, etc.:

Forecastle	Red
Top	White
Quarterdeck	Blue
Engine Room	Green
Royal Marines	Black
Signal	Yellow

Deck Cloths on Upper Deck.—The following routine is carried out with deck cloths on Upper Deck:

(*a*) *At the Pipe 'Dry down the Upper Deck'*—All doors to the Embrasures and Daylight Workshop flat are to be closed until deck cloths have been placed on the dried decks concerned.

(*b*) *Daily at* 0855 (*except Saturday*) *and* 1550 (*Evening Quarters*):
2 Torpedo ratings make up deck cloths in Workshop Flat.
4 Forecastlemen (2 each side) make up deck cloths in Embrasures.
4 Topmen (2 each side) make up deck cloths at fore end of Batteries.
Leading Hand of Scullery Party is responsible that Galley and Preparing Room doors are closed at these times.
The Captain of the Side is responsible that the shute is closed at these times.
After Commander's Rounds at 0905 (*after Divisions on Sundays*) *and* 1600—*the above parties Down deck cloths, open doors and shute.*

(*c*) *Ship open to Visitors.*—Deck cloths on U.D. will normally be kept up during the time ship is open to visitors.

11. ORGANISATION FOR CLEANING SHIP BELOW

Note.

Compartments or spaces not mentioned below are looked after by the department using them.

Requirements of Sweepers from Parts of Ship.

F.X.	Cable Locker Flat				1	
	Sick Bay Flat				1	
	Heads				1 A.B.	
			(Head Party do Heads Flat)			
	Reading Room and Dental Flat			1		
	Issue Room Flat				1	
	Messdeck				1	
	A Space				1	
	Approaches to 95, etc.				–	
		Total			7	

Top	Starb. Amm. Passage (133–217)		1	
	C.P.O.'s and P.O.'s Bathroom.		1	
	Seamen's Bathroom		2	
	Messdeck		1	
	Drying Room		1	
	Heads		1 A.B. and 1 L.S.	
	Engineer's Office Flat (217–248)		–	
	Total		7	

Q.D.	C.P.O.'s Flat					1
	Hammock Flat					1
	Messdeck					1
	G.R. Flat					1
	15-in. T.S.					1
	Approach to Y Handing Room			–	
	Heads					1
		Total			6	

Boatswain's Party.

Approaches to Painted Canvas Store and Sand Tank.

Spaces cleaned by other Departments or Parties

Gunner's Party.

Fore and After 5.5-in. Space, 5.5-in. Magazines and Shell Rooms, and all Magazines (except Warhead and 15-in.).

EXECUTIVE ORGANISATION

Torpedo Party.
All Stores and Magazines under Torpedo Flats, A.W. Flat, P. and S., Main Switchboard Room, Spare Armature Rooms and Lobbies and Approaches, Approach to Gunner (T.'s) Store (aft), After Generator Flat, Main Telephone Exchange, Nos. 1 and 2 L.P. Rooms and Lobbies outside, L.P. Generator Rooms, P. and S., both Gyro Rooms, Warhead Magazine.

Turrets' Crews.
Shell Rooms, Shell Handing Rooms, Cordite Handing Rooms.

Royal Marines.
Office Flat, Boat Hoist Flat, Starb. Amm. Passage, Stewards' Flat, Central Store Space, 280 to Stern both sides, 'X' Space, W.R. Bathroom, G.R. Bathroom, W.O.'s Bathroom and Round House, Midshipmen's Chest Flat (Band) and Chapel, Captain's Lobby Flat, Officers' Baggage Store, Starb. A.W. Torpedo Flat, Schoolroom Flat.

E.R. Department.
Port Amm. Passage (133–280), Approaches to Compartments used by E.R. Department.

Chief Q.M.
Chart and Chronometer Room, Lower Steering Position and Lower Conning Tower.

Captain's Coxswain.
Lobby to Admiral's and Captain's Store Rooms.

M.A.A.
Cells and Scran Bag.

Paymaster's Party.
Approaches to Cold Chamber, 95–105 Port, Paymaster's Store (Port) and Provision Room (Port), Leather Store and No. 11 Store.
S.A.P.—One hand from each part (standing numbers) fallen out whenever possible.

Store Room Approach Party.
Approaches to Clothing Issue Room and Lamp Room, etc. Awning Room, etc. 95–105 Starb. Main Deck to Lower Deck, Spirit Room Flat, Officers' Bedding Store, W.O.'s Store, W.R. and G.R. Stores.

Sick Berth Staff.
Fore Medical Distribution Station.

Barge's Crew.
After Medical Distribution Station.

Admiral's Office Orderlies.
Staff Office.

RULINGS

Electric Light Fittings.

Torpedo Party clean inside of globes and bulbs.

Department concerned cleans outside of globes.

The whole of electric light fittings in cabins and messes will be cleaned by specially detailed Torpedo ratings.

Rulings for:

CLEANING SCUTTLES

All Flat sweepers and Ward Room Officers' Attendants who have scuttles in the particular part of the ship, for the cleanliness of which they are responsible, are to examine the same at 0830 *Every Morning*, and where necessary, they are to be cleaned by 0900.

Scuttles are always to be cleaned after rain or rough weather.

N.B.—The parts which show from outboard are:

(*a*) The ring in the ship's side.

(*b*) The brass ring securing the rubber.

Rulings for:

CLEANING OF HATCHWAYS, WATER-TIGHT DOORS, LADDERS, ETC.

Hatchways and Water-tight Doors separating one compartment from another, are to be kept clean as follows:

The Hatch or Water-tight Door is to be considered as Shut. The Part of Ship or Department on either side cleans all on its own side of the compartment. This includes all approaches. The under side of the Hatch or the closing side of the Doors includes the rubber.

12. TABLE OF SPECIAL DUTIES

PARTY	F.X.		TOP		Q.D.		BOYS	
Messmen:	P.O.'s	6	W.O.'s	2	G.R. Pantry	1	Instr. Mess	1
	Sick Bay	1	Cooks	1	O.A. & E.A.'s	4		
	C.P.O. Writers	1	S.A.'s	1	C.P.O.'s	2		
	G.R. Pantry	2			M.A.A.	1		
					R.P.O.'s	1		
					Admiral's Stewards	1		
		10		4		10		1
Sweepers:	Messdeck	1	Messdeck	1	Messdeck	1	Messdeck	2
	Sick Bay Flat	2	C. & P.O. Bath	1	C.P.O.'s Flat	2	Boys' Bath	2
	Cable Locker Flat	1	Seamen's Bath	3	G.R. Flat	1	Issue Room Flat	1
	Reading Room	1	Drying Room	1	Eng. Off. Flat.	1	'A' Space	1
	Nav. Yeoman	2	Bath Rm. Flat	1				
			Band Flat	1				
		7		8		5		6
Gunnery Sweepers:	'A' Turret	3	'B' Turret	3	'Y' Turret	3		
	5.5-in. Guns	3	5.5-in. Guns	3	5.5-in. Guns	3		
	Stb. Pom-Pom	1	Port Pom-Pom	1	4-in. Guns	2		
	15-in. Top	1	G.C.T.	1	H.A.C.R.	1		
	15-in. T.S.	1	Q.O.'s	3	Q.O.'s.	4		
	Q.O.'s	4						
		13		11		13		

12. Table of Special Duties—*continued*

Composite Parties	F.X.	Top	Q.D.	Boys
Gunner's	2	2	1	–
Boatswain's	–	2	–	2
Shipwright's	1	–	–	–
Side	2	2	2	–
Head	1	1	2	–
Painting	1	1	2	–
Boat	1	1	1	5
Double Bottom	1	1	1	–
Central Store	1	–	1	–
Captain's Cabin	1	–	–	–
Admiral's Cabin	–	1	2	–
Barge's Crew	1	2	1	–
S.E.O.'s Boat	1	1	–	–
Victualling Party	–	–	3	–
Scullery	–	4	–	–
Store Room Approach	1	–	–	–
Painter's Mate	–	–	1	–
Sailmaker's Mate	–	–	1	–
Telephone Exchange	1	2	1	–
Writers	–	1	–	–
Acting Schoolmaster	–	1	–	–
Buglers	–	1	–	1
	15	23	19	9
Grand total	46	46	46	44

(Including Messengers.)

Messengers:

Captain	1	Boy
Commander	1	Ord. (F.X.)
Captain's Office	1	Boy
Commander's Office	1	”
Gunnery Office	1	”
Staff Office	1	”
Boys' Office	1	”
Pool	2	Boys
S.D.O.	4	” (on cruises when insufficient Signal Boys are borne)

Side Boys . . . 3 ⎫
Call-boys . . . 4 ⎬ In each Watch
O.O.W. . . . 1 ⎭

Total . . . 29

13. EXCUSED LIST

'CLEAR LOWER DECK.'—NO ONE IS EXCUSED 'CLEAR LOWER DECK' EXCEPT RATINGS ON WATCH.

Ex.—Excused.   Att.—Attends.

	CLEAN SHIP				Divisions	Watch	Quarters	Watch of Hands	Entering and Leaving Harbour	Sea Tricks
	Hands Fall in	Scrub Decks Till	Clean Guns	Clean Messdeck						
Bathroom Sweepers	Att.	B.	Att.	Ex.	Ex. D.N.	Ex. A.	Att.	Att.	Att.	Att.
Boatswain's Mates	Ex.	Ex.	Att. W.	—	Att. W.	Ex.	Att. W.	Ex.	Att. W.	—
Boatswain's Party	Att.	B.	Att.	Att.	Ex. D.N.	Ex. A.	Att.	Att.	Att.	Att.
Buglers	Ex.	Ex.	Att. W.	Att. W.	Att.	Ex.	Att.	Ex.	Att.	—
Cabin Hands	Att.	Ex.	Ex.	Ex.	Ex.	Ex.	Ex.	Ex.	Ex.	Ex.
Central Store Party	Att.	B.	Att.	Ex. D.N.	Ex. D.N.	Ex. A.	Att.	Att.	Att.	Ex. A.
Control Sweepers	Att.	B.	Att.	Att.	Ex. D.N.	Ex. A.	Att.	Att.	Ex.	Ex.
Double Bottom Party	Ex.	Work with E.R. Dept.		Ex.	Ex. N.	—	Att.	Ex.	Ex.	Ex.
Drying Room	Att.	0630	Ex.	Ex.	Att.	Ex.	Att.	Ex. after 1600–2100	Att.	Ex. until 2200
Duty Boat's Crews (Not Power Boats)	Att.	Boats	Att. U.C.	Att. U.C.	Att. U.	Att. U.	Att. U.M.	Att. U.	Att.	Att.
Gun Sweepers	Att.	B.	Att.	Att.	Att.	Att.	Att.	Att.	Att.	Att.
Gunner's Party	Att.	B. Y.	Att.	Att. Y.	Ex. D.N.	Ex. A.	Att.	Att.	Att. Y.	Att.
Head Party	Att.	Heads	Ex. S.	Ex.	Ex. D.N.	Ex. A.	Att.	Att.	Att.	Ex. A. L.
Mates—Blacksmith's	Att.	B.	Att.	Att.	Ex. D.N.	Ex. A.	Att.	0830 only Ex. A.L.	Att.	Ex. A.
" Painter's	Att.	B.	Att.	Att.	Ex. D.N.	Ex. A.	Att.	Att.	Att.	Ex. A.
" Sailmaker's	Att.	B.	Att.	Att.	Ex. D.N.	Ex. A.	Att.	Att.	Att.	Ex. A.
Messdeck and Flat Sweepers	Att.	B.	Att.	Att.	Ex. D.N.	Ex. A.	Att.	Att.	Att.	Att.
Messmen	Att.	0630	Att.*	Att.	Ex. D.N.	Ex.	Att.	Ex.	Att. M.	Ex.

Messengers	Att.	B.	Att.	Att.W.	Ex.D.N.	Ex.A.	Att.	Ex.A.	Att.	Ex.A.L.
Navigator's Yeoman	Att.	B.	Att.	Att.	Att.	Ex.A.	Att.	Att.	Att.	Att.
Power Boats (Duty Crews)	Att.	Boats	Boats	Ex.	Ex.D.N.	Ex.	Ex.	Ex.	Att.	Att.
Power Boats (Stand off Crews)	Ex.	Ex.	Att.	Att.	Att.		Att.	Ex.	Att.	Att.
Q.O.'s	Att.	B.	Att.	Ex.N.	Ex.D.N.	Ex.A.	Att.	Ex.A.	Att.	Ex.A.
Quartermasters	Ex.	—	Att.W.	Att.W.	Ex.D.N.	Ex.A.	Ex.N.	Ex.	Ex.N.	
Shipwright's Party	Att.	B.	Att.	Ex.N.	Ex.D.N.	Ex.A.	Att.	Att.	Att.	Ex.A.
Scullery Party	Att.	B.	Ex.	Ex.	Ex.D.N.	Ex.A.L.	Ex.	0830 only	Ex.	Ex.A.L.
Side Boys and Messengers	Att.		Boys' Orders	Boys' Orders	Att.W.	Ex.	Att.W.	Att.W.	Att.W.	Att.
Side Party	Att.	B.	Att.	Att.S.N.	Ex.D.N.	Ex.A.	Att.	Att.	Att.	Att.
Special Painting Party	Att.	B.	Att.	Att.	Ex.D.N.	Ex.A.	Att.	Att.	Att.	Att.
Store Room Approach Party	Att.	B.	Att.	Att.	Ex.D.N.	Ex.A.	Att.	Att.	Att.	Att.
Telephone Exchange	Ex.	Ex.	Att.W.	Att.W.	Att.W.	Ex.	Att.W.	Ex.	Att.W.	S.S.
Torpedo Party	Att.	S.S.	Att.	Att.	Ex.	Ex.A.	Att.	Ex. 2030	Att.	Ex.A.
Training Classes	Att.	B.	Att.	Att.	Ex.	Ex.A.	Att.	Att.	Att.	Ex.A.L.
Turret Sweepers	Att.	B.	Att.	Att.	Ex.D.N.	Ex.A.	Att.	0830 only	Ex.	Ex.A.
Victualling Party	Att.	B.	Att.	Ex.	Ex.D.N.	Ex.A.L.	Att.	Att.	Att.	Ex.
Writers (Cdr. and G.I.)	Att.	Ex.	Att.	Ex.	Ex.D.N.	Ex.	Att.	Ex.	Att.	

A.—Except after working hours.
L.—Except after working hours and until after 2000.
W.—Except when on watch.
U.—Unless actually away.
M.—Excused from ½ hour before to ½ hour after a meal.
D.—Except on Drill Days.
*.—Messes with more than one Messman, half attend Clean Guns, all attend on Saturday.

C.—Except when cleaning.
S.—Except on Saturday.
N.—Except on Sunday.
Y.—Gunner's Yeoman excused.
B.—Breakfast.
S.S.—Special Stations.

WORKING HOURS END AT—1600 Ordinary Days.
1200 Make-and-Mend Days.
Divisions on Sundays.

14. TYPICAL PROCEDURE FOR DETAILING
WORKING PARTIES

(1) *Signal.*—'A Working Party of 1 P.O. and 20 A.B.'s is to be provided to clear up R.N. Canteen, A.M. Thursday, 8th June. Party should report to Warrant M.A.A. of Greenwich.'

(2) *Signal Distribution.*—Signal goes to Commander's Office.

(3) *In Commander's Office.*—Contents of Signal noted in Diary. Regulating C.P.O. in Commander's Office consults Diary to see outstanding commitments for Thursday, 8th, and sees F.X. are ranging cable. He also consults weekly 'G.' and 'T.' programmes to see what drills are on that day.

(4) *Action for Detailing.*—Commander's Office sends chits to the Officers of F.X., Top and Q.D. Divisions, stating that 4 F.X., 10 Top and 6 Q.D. are required for R.N. Canteen W.P. A.M. Thursday, 8th June, not to be taken from H.A. Control Parties. Commander's Office details suitable P.O. from Watch Bill.

(5) *Action by Division.*—Each Division details its own men, and then sends list to Commander's Office, giving names and messes of men detailed.

Commander's Office compiles list for P.O. in charge, and to Victualling Office (if required).

(6) *Daily Orders.*—Extract of Daily Orders, Thursday, 8th June:

> *Extra Parties:*
>
> > 0825.   R.N. Canteen W.P.   1 P.O. and 20.
> > Dress No. 5's.   Take overall suits.
>
> *Boats:*
>
> > 0835.   Boat to take R.N. Canteen W.P. to Rosyth.
> > 1130.   Boat to fetch R.N. Canteen W.P. from Rosyth.'

15. WATER-TIGHT DOORS

(1) *General.*—The term 'door' includes W.T. Hatches, Scuttles, and Valves.

(2) *Category of Doors:*

> 'C' Doors are those which are always closed at sea and in harbour, except when access to the compartment is required.
>
> 'B' Doors are those which are closed at sea, and at night in harbour, except when required for access by men working or watch-keeping in the compartment.
>
> 'A' Doors are those normally open for access throughout the ship, only being closed at Collision Stations.

(3) *Unauthorised Persons.*—No unauthorised person is to open or close a W.T. Door.

(4) *Closing W.T. Doors.*—No man is to close a W.T. Door without first making sure that all drain valves, ventilating valves, etc., which can be worked only from inside the compartment are closed. Ventilating Fans inside the compartment must be stopped. If this order cannot be or, for good reason, is not carried out, the fact is to be reported to a responsible officer and the O.O.W.

(5) *Reporting Closing of W. T. Doors.*—Whenever W.T. Doors are closed for Collision Stations or by pipe, reports are to be made to the Executive Officer, as well as the O.O.W.

(6) *Opening W. T. Doors.*—'A' and 'B' Doors. When 'A' and 'B' Doors are closed, they are not to be opened until piped, except by permission of O.O.W.

'C' Doors are never to be opened at sea, except after permission has been obtained in person from O.O.W.

Ventilating Valves and Magazine Cooling System (which are only to be worked by E.R. Department) and 'B' Doors to the E.R. Department spaces may be opened under charge of the Engineer Officer of Watch, who is to inform O.O.W. by chit at beginning of each watch, what doors under his charge are open.

Other 'B' Doors may be opened by permission of O.O.W., whose permission can be sought by telephone.

(7) *Water-tight Door Book.*—In harbour, between 2030 and 0645, the O.O.W., and at sea at all times, the Midshipman of the Watch aft, is to keep a record in the Water-tight Door Book of all 'B' and 'C' Doors, with the exception of the special Engine Room doors (*vide* list in Water-tight Door Book), for which permission has been given: O.O.W. is to initial the book at the end of each watch.

(8) *Inspection of W. T. Doors at Sea.*—A P.O. or Leading Seaman in each part of ship is to go rounds once during each watch to ascertain that no doors are open, other than those shown in the book. No door need be opened for the purpose of inspecting a door in a lower compartment.

Result of these inspections is to be entered in O.O.W.'s Book, and signed by the rating.

Ratings carrying out these rounds are also to take note and report if it appears necessary to close any ventilating valves, hatches or skylights on account of bad weather.

(9) *Closing 'B' and 'C' Doors. Entering or Leaving Harbour.*—For closing 'B' and 'C' Doors and all scuttles for entering or leaving harbour, men will be detailed by Captains of Tops under Officers of Divisions, with the exception of Officers' Quarters, where the scuttles will be closed by the Wardroom Attendants and Cabin Hands.

WATER-TIGHT DOORS.   ALLOCATION

The ship is divided for the purposes of closing water-tight doors as follows:

F.X. Upper deck
Main deck   } From Stem to 133 Station.
Lower deck and below

Top Upper deck
Main deck   } From 133 to 217 Station.
Lower deck and below

Q.D. Upper deck from 217 Station to Stern.
Main deck from 280 Station to Stern.
Lower deck and below 280 Station to Stern both sides.

UPPER DECK AND ABOVE		MAIN DECK		LOWER DECK AND BELOW	
Station	Part	Station	Part	Station	Part
Stem to 133	F.X.	Stem to 133	F.X.	Stem to 133	F.X.
133 to 217	Top	280 to Stern	Q.D.	280 to Stern	Q.D.
217 to Stern	Q.D.	133 to 280	E.R.	133 to 280	E.R.

16. SEA DUTIES

General.—(1) At sea, the Watch on Deck is to be the Duty Part of a Watch.

(2) Between 2130 and Hands fall in next morning, No man of the Watch on Deck is to go below without permission. At other times, men not otherwise required on deck may go below to the messdecks.

(2*a*) Sea Dutymen are detailed as follows:

Helmsmen	F.X. 1
Telegraphsmen . . .	Q.D. 1
Flagmen	Q.D. 2
Conemen	Top 2
Bridge Telephones . .	Top 2
Bridge Messengers . .	F.X. 2
Seaman Gunner of Watch .	Gunnery Office
Rangetaker of Watch . .	Gunnery Office
Rangefinder Trainer . .	Gunnery Office
Special Leadsman (Starboard)	F.X. } Boatswain's
Special Leadsman (Port) .	Top } Mates

These ratings are divided between the three parts of ship. When requiring reliefs, they inform their Divisional Petty Officers, who details one, consulting Gunnery Office as necessary.

(2*b*) The following Sea Dutymen closed up during a Make-

and-Mend are to be given a Make-and-Mend the following Weekday in lieu:

> Helmsmen.
>
> Telegraphsmen.
>
> Rangetakers and Rangefinder Trainers of the Watch.

(2c) Except as above, all Sea Dutymen are to work part of the ship when not closed up.

(3) *Special Sea Dutymen.*—Special Sea Dutymen are the Sea Dutymen (*vide* Station Board) for the Duty and Non-Duty Part of the Watch on Deck.

In addition, the Chief Q.M. goes to the wheel, one Q.M. to the Lower Conning Tower and one to the Quarterdeck.

(4) Ordinary Sea Dutymen calls Sea Dutymen of the Watch on Deck (*i.e.* Duty Part) only. Between sunset and sunrise, Sea Dutymen are to include a Searchlight's Crew.

(5) Special Sea Dutymen are to be piped to their Stations twenty minutes before weighing, slipping, anchoring or securing.

(6) *Tricks.*—The Petty Officer of the Watch on Deck is to organise tricks as follows:

POSITION	RATING	DURATION
Masthead Lookout	1 O.S. or Boy	1 hour trick during daylight.
Compass Platform	2 O.S. or Boys	1 hour trick during darkness.
Helm	Ord. Seamen	1 hour tricks.

(7) The Q.M. is to record in a book the names of all Ordinary Seamen who do a trick at the wheel.

(8) *Sea Boat's Crew and Lowerers.*—Sea Boat's Crew and Lowerers are to be detailed from each Part of the Watch and shown on the Sea Duties List.

(9) The first Sea Boat's Crew consists of Crew and Lowerers from the Part of Watch on Deck, and they are never to go below the Upper Deck, or before No. 2 Breakwater, or abaft P. 1 and S. 1 Guns unless specially ordered to do so by the O.O.W.

During working hours, Sea Boat's Crew and Lowerers are to be employed by their Divisional Petty Officers, subject to the above restrictions.

(10) The second Sea Boat's Crew consists of Crew and Lowerers from the Non-Duty Part of the Watch on Deck, and they are alway to be piped to fall in whenever the first Sea Boat's Crew is called away.

(11) The term *Life Boat's Crew* is to be used if a boat is called away to save life, and in all cases the boat to be manned is always to be named.

(12) When exercising, the pipe is to be 'Sea Boat's Crew fall in abreast ——Boat.'

(13) On mustering the Sea Boat's Crew at the beginning of each Watch, a warning notice of their restrictions, printed on a board, is to be read to them.

(14) Sea Boat's Crews are to be mustered once without warning in every night watch.

(15) *Sounding Party.*—Members of the Sea Boat's Crew are to be detailed to rig, work and unrig Sounding Booms.

(16) *Fog Stations.*—A Fog Buoy is always to be ready for streaming when in company at sea, and if streamed, a second buoy is to be provided at once. Sea Boat's Crew are to be used to stream Fog Buoy.

(17) Fog Lookouts are to be detailed as follows:

> (*a*) A Petty Officer and 2 men right forward, one man to man the direct telephone in the Head hatch, one man to have a megaphone.
>
> (*b*) Signalmen aloft to supplement Mastheadman.
>
> (*c*) 1 Leading Seaman and 2 men right aft, one man at the direct telephone.

F.X. are to supply the 2 men right forward and Q.D. the 2 men right aft.

The P.O. and Leading Seamen are to be supplied by each part of the ship in turn.

Top are to take over Masthead Lookouts.

(18) A searchlight is to be manned when Fog Lookouts are placed.

(19) A Signalman is to be sent aft with Speed Flags.

(20) *Oil Navigation Lights.*—At sunset, oil navigation lights, burning, are to be placed as follows and reported to the O.O.W.

Light	Responsible	Placed		Remarks	
Fore Steaming	F.X.	Galley Flat		Container only	
Port Bow	Top	"	"	"	"
Starboard Bow	Top	"	"	"	"
Stern	Q.D.	Signal D.O.			
N.U.C. Lights	Q.D.	"	"		

17. DUTY HANDS

(1) If a few hands are required in working hours, '2 hands from each part of ship and a Leading Hand F.X. (or Top or Q.D.)' will normally be piped.

(2) If a few hands are required in non-working hours, the Duty Hands are to be used. They consist of 1 Leading Seaman and 6 hands, and form part of the Emergency Party (see Article No. 18). The seamen will be detailed equally from each part of

ship and are to be taken in rotation from all seamen except the following:

Torpedo Party	Watch-keepers
Office Writers	Duty Boats' Crews
Cabin Hands	Drying Room Sweeper

(3) Captains of Tops are to hand in a list to Commander's Office by Saturday noon, giving names of their Duty Hands for forthcoming week and Commander's Office will compile a complete list. The Leading Hand will be detailed through Commander's Office.

(4) Duty Hands will work from noon to noon, and will be available for work as required.

18. EMERGENCY PARTY IN HARBOUR

(1) *Duties of Emergency Party.*—The Emergency Party is composed of Seamen and Marines from the Duty Part of the Watch and performs the following duties:

(a) Provides Seamen and Marines for the Fire Party.
(b) Provides Night Boat's Crew and Lowerers.
(c) Provides Anchor Watch when required.
(d) Provides the Duty Hands and Hammock Stowers.
(e) Performs any unexpected work out of working hours.

(2) *Detailing Emergency Party.*—The party is to be detailed daily in harbour from the Duty Part of the Watch of Hands, taken from all hands in rotation, and is to commence duty at 1200 daily.

(3) *Composition of Emergency Party:*

PERSONNEL	SLEEPING BILLET
1 Petty Officer	Tallied Hammock
2 Leading Seamen	Tallied Hammocks in
6 Seamen from each part of ship	Gunroom Flat
1 N.C.O.	Tallied Hammocks in
4 Royal Marines	special billets

(4) *Mustering Emergency Party:*

1145. Muster with the Fire Party of the duty part, prior to commencing duty at 1200.

2045. Muster, and detail Night Boat's Crew and Lowerers, and report at night rounds. Boat is to be rigged before rounds and unrigged before hands fall in in the morning.

(5) *Night Searchlight's Crew.*—Consisting of 1 L.S. and 2 A.B.'s of the Torpedo Party. They muster at 2045 with the Emergency Party.

19. FIRE PARTY

There is a Fire Party detailed from each part of the Watch, and doing duty from 1200–1200 each day.

Composition of Fire Party:
- (*a*) Duty Lieutenant-Commander.
- (*b*) Duty Engineer Officer.
- (*c*) Duty Warrant Officer.
- (*d*) Duty Gunner's Mate.
- (*e*) Duty Petty Officer.
- (*f*) Seamen and Marines of Emergency Party.
- (*g*) Torpedo Fire Party of 1 P.O., 1 L.S. and 4 hands.
- (*h*) Duty Hand of Gunner's Party (Smoke Helmet).
- (*i*) Duty Shipwright and Duty Artisan.
- (*j*) Two E.R.A.'s (Flooding Keys).
- (*k*) Stokers Fire Party of 1 S.P.O., 1 Leading Stoker, and 6 Stokers.
- (*l*) Bugler.

Mustering Fire Party.—The Fire Party of the Duty Part of the Watch takes over duty at 1200, and is to muster at 1145 daily, under Duty Lieutenant-Commander.

20. SLINGING BILLETS

1. Midshipmen . . .	Warrant Officers' Flat and After Cabin Flats.
2. Chief and Petty Officers.	In Messes.
3. F.X.	Messdeck.
4. Topmen	Messdeck.
5. Q.D.	Messdeck and Port Ammunition Passage Aft.
6. Torpedomen . . .	Messdeck and Daylight Workshop.
7. Junior Accountant Ratings	Messdeck.
8. Stokers	Messdeck.
9. Royal Marines . . .	Messdeck and Starboard Ammunition Passage.
10. Boys	Messdeck.
11. Signal and W/T. Ratings.	Messdeck.
12. Men under punishment .	Port Ammunition Passage After end.
13. Emergency party and N.B. Crew	Outside Gunroom.
14. Watch-keepers. . .	Starboard Ammunition Passage After end.

The following is an amplification of the above:

Box Messes	Ratings occupying messes.
Issue Room Flat (from 133 bulkhead forward)	Boys.
Upper Deck Starboard (133 bulkhead to entrance to Boat Hoist Flat) . .	Boys.
Main deck Starboard (133 bulkhead to 280 bulkhead)	Royal Marines and R.M. Band.
Boat Hoist Flat	Royal Marines and R.M. Band.

Upper Deck Port (196 bulkhead to entrance to Gunroom Flat)	Q.O.'s, Torpedomen, Quarter deckmen.
Main Deck Port (133 bulkhead to 280 bulkhead)	
Stokers' Upper Messdeck (from Armour bulkhead to 133 Port)	Stokers.
Stokers' Lower Messdeck (from 101 to 133 bulkheads each side)	
Boys	Boys' Messdeck.
Gun Room Flat	Night Boat's Crew and Emergency Party.
Sick Bay Flat	Boys.
Upper Deck Port (133 bulkhead to 196 bulkhead)	Shpts. Ch. Sto. and S.P.O.'s Messes. Overflow O.A.'s, E.A.'s and E.R.A.'s.

Notes.

(1) Gangways outside Box messes, and on Messdecks are to be left clear of hammocks as far as possible.

(2) No hammocks are to be slung in Above Water Flats.

(3) No hammocks are to be slung in Dental Flat.

21. HAMMOCKS

(1) Hammock Stowers are to be the Emergency Party, and they alone are to hand out or stow hammocks.

(2) No hammock is to be stowed unless properly lashed up with seven equidistant turns.

(3) Hammocks are to be stowed vertically, with a layer of horizontal hammocks underneath, where necessary.

(4) Hammock Stowers are to restow libertymen's hammocks after others are down, and on Friday evenings are to sweep out the nettings.

(5) In the morning, the Duty Petty Officer is to report to the O.O.W. when hammocks are stowed, after which the Petty Officer of Messdeck is responsible until 'Stand by Hammocks.'

All Guard and Steerage Hammocks are to be stowed by 0645.

(6) From the time hammocks are stowed until 'Stand by Hammocks,' no man is to take out his hammock without permission from the Petty Officer of the Messdeck, except libertymen on nights when clean hammocks are slung. This regulation is to prevent other men's hammocks being disturbed and becoming dirty or wet on the decks.

(7) Clean hammocks will as a rule be slung on alternate Fridays. Libertymen are to sling clean hammocks before they go.

(8) Hammocks will be scrubbed the following Monday or Tuesday. The usual five stops, and method of securing to gantlines (named up and inboard) are to be employed.

(9) When scrubbed hammocks are being got up, all Captains of Parts are to attend.

22. CABLE PARTY

(1) A Cable Party is detailed from each Watch as follows:

On F.X.:   1 P.O. (Captain of F.X.)

1 Leading Seaman.

2 A.B.'s and 1 Ord., from each part of ship.

1 Shipwright.

1 Chief Stoker or Stoker P.O., for working Capstan Engine.

1 Blacksmith.

1 Signal rating.

1 Torpedo rating, for F.X. phone.

Cable Locker: 1 N.C.O. and 8 men in each watch for stowing the cable.

Note.—The Captain of F.X. is to be in Cable Party of Starboard Watch.

(2) If the hands do not go to Stations for Entering Harbour, the Cable Party of the Watch on Deck will bring the ship to an anchor. When hands do go to Stations for Entering Harbour, the Cable Party of the Starboard Watch will be on the Forecastle and in the Cable Locker.

(3) If the job (*e.g.* Mooring) requires more than the above, the Cable Party of the Port Watch will also be piped.

ANCHOR WATCH

(1) *Emergency Party—Clearing Away.*—If an Anchor Watch is required, the Emergency Party is to fall in and clear away cables as necessary, Marines in Cable Locker.

(2) *Anchor Watch—Detailing.*—The Anchor Watch is to be detailed from the Emergency Party and is to consist of:

1 P.O. (or Leading Seaman).

2 A.B.'s.

1 A.B. (on Bridge phone).

1 Shipwright.

1 (T.) rating with lights on F.X.

(3) *Steam on Main Engines.*—If steam is on the Main Engines, the following will be required in addition:

Q.M. at Wheel.

1 Telegraphsman.

1 E.R. rating for Capstan.

(4) *O.O.W.*—Will keep watch on the Bridge. He will satisfy himself that the Anchor Watch knows exactly what to do if ordered to let go anchor.

23. PRECAUTIONARY MEASURES

(1) *Going Aloft.*—No one is to go aloft above the Tops without first obtaining the O.O.W.'s permission.

(2) *Working over the Side at Sea.*—No one is to work outboard of the guardrails at sea, unless by O.O.W.'s order, or unless his permission has been obtained. Each man is to be in a bowline constantly attended.

(3) *Working over the Side in a Tideway or Bad Weather.*—Men working outside the guard rails in a tideway or bad weather are to wear bowlines.

(4) *Funnels.*—Men are not to be triced up to Funnels until O.O.W. has ascertained from E.R. Department that it is safe to do so.

(5) *Confined Spaces.*—No one, not belonging to E.R. Department, is to attempt to enter a confined space or compartment, without first obtaining permission from the Engineer Commander or his representative. A safety lamp is to be lowered first and is to be seen burning brightly before a man enters the space.

(6) *Unshipping Ladders.*—Whenever a ladder or hatch is removed, the ladderway or hatchway is to be properly roped off.

(7) *Boats for Bathers* are always to have a coxswain and a lifebuoy.

(8) *Shooting Parties.*—The officer or coxswain in charge of a boat is always to enquire of officers returning from shooting parties if their guns are unloaded when they enter the boat. Officers coming on board the ship with guns are to show them broken to the O.O.W. as they come over the side.

(9) *Guardrails.*—The pins of upper guardrails are always to be in place.

The Boatswain is to inspect guardrails daily at Evening Quarters, and on proceeding to sea, and is to make a report to the Commander.

24. BOATS—GENERAL

There is no truer saying than the old one that 'A Ship is known by her Boats.'

Appearance of Ship.—Midshipmen and coxswains of boats under way are to scrutinise their ship and any irregularity, such as anything hanging over the side or from scuttles, boats not square, washed clothes hung in an improper place, etc., is to be reported to the Officer of Watch.

Boat-keepers.—Boats at the booms are to have a boat-keeper in them, unless, due to wind or tide, orders are given to the contrary. These boat-keepers are to keep their boats clean and shipshape.

They are to stand and salute at 'Colours,' 'Sunset' or when officers are passing.

They are to be detailed in rotation by coxswains of boats.

Boat-ropes.—The coxswain of a boat leaving the boom is responsible for the boat-rope being hauled taut.

Capacity of Drifter and Boats:

BOAT	DAY WEATHER		NIGHT WEATHER	
	Fair	*Foul*	*Fair*	*Foul*
Drifter	350	275	262	206
1st Launch	150	100	112	75
2nd Launch	110	70	82	52
Picquet Boat	35	28	26	21
Motor Boat	20	15	15	11
Cutter	45	30	33	22
Gig	15	10	11	7
Whaler	12	8	9	6
Skiff	5	0	3	0

Church Pendant in Ships.—Boats are not to come alongside aft when the Church Pendant is flying for Church or Prayers.

Conduct of Boats.—(*a*) No boat is to lie alongside a gangway or inshore unless ordered to do so.

(*b*) Power boats, when coming alongside, should never have to resort to 'Full Astern.' Steerage way only is necessary.

(*c*) Boats are to give a wide berth round the bows or sterns of ships and are to keep out of the way of ships under way.

Conduct of Crews under Way.—When under way crews are to remain in their appointed places and are not to lounge about.

Boats are not to be scrubbed out or bright-work cleaned when under way.

Defects and Losses.—Any defects or losses are to be reported to the Commander and Boat Officer at the first opportunity.

Dress of Boats' Crews.—Crews must invariably be dressed alike. Particular attention should be given to oilskins, chinstays and boots. Chinstays are to be worn down. Stoker Petty Officers and Stokers in power boats are to wear a blue overall suit with a cap (and cap ribbon in the latter case).

Gear to be in Boats.—Boats are always to carry an anchor, grapnel, boat's bag and lead line. In addition, duty boats are to have a lantern and compass. Motor power boats are to carry a Pyrene fire extinguisher. Boats are to carry a signal book, Answering Pendant and a set of hand flags.

Hooking on, etc.—If boat-keepers of a boat are called away (for hooking on or shifting the boat) the following numbers are required:

Cutters: Coxswain and 3 hands.

Gigs and Whalers: Coxswain and 2 hands.

Skiffs: 1 hand.

Jacob's Ladders.—There is no objection to the bottoms of Jacob's Ladders being turned up to avoid damage to paintwork when a boat is at the boom, but the coxswain is to see that they are left hanging straight when his boat leaves the boom.

Libertymen and Lifebuoys.—All boats carrying libertymen are to have lifebuoys ready for use.

Lowering Boats.—Boats are not to be lowered with less than two hands on each fall, or in the case of a sea-boat three hands on each fall and a Petty Officer in charge.

Oars in Pulling Boats.—Oars in pulling boats are to be told off and marked for their proper thwart.

Pulling Boats after Dark.—Pulling boats away after dark are to carry a light on the stanchion aft.

Salutes from Boats.—Midshipmen and coxswains of boats are to acquaint themselves with salutes from boats and ensure the appropriate marks of respect are paid.

Signals—Lookout for.—A sharp lookout for signals is to be kept when away from the ship. Coxswains of boats are reminded that proficiency in reading signals is a part of their duty.

Signal Lights—Use of, in Distress.—Power boats are to carry a signal pistol and 12 signal lights of each colour. The following code is to be employed:

(*a*) Succession of Red Lights: Am in distress and require immediate assistance.

(*b*) Succession of Green Lights: Am broken down or aground and require assistance, but situation is not serious at present.

(*c*) Succession of White Lights: Assistance is no longer required.

Smart Manning of Boats.—(1) Boats are to be manned smartly and crews are to run out along the booms. Boats are to be pulled and not hauled to the gangway.

(2) Depending on the nature of the boat trip and other circumstances at the time, it is to be left to the discretion of the O.O.W. at what time the boat should be called away.

(3) Normally boats should be called away 10 minutes before they are required to leave the ship.

Smoking not Allowed.—On no account is smoking ever to be allowed in boats, except when a boat is away on a prolonged duty and is clear of Fleet Anchorage and landing-places.

Sporting Guns in Boats.—Officers carrying rifles or guns are always to be asked if these are unloaded before the weapon is brought into the boat.

Staff Officers—Boats for.—The Captain's motor boat is available for use by Staff Officers. The procedure is that the Staff Officer obtains the Captain's permission to use the boat and then informs the Officer of Watch of the time the boat is required. If the

Captain's motor boat is not available, ship's boats are to give every assistance.

Steaming Lights.—Steaming lights for all power boats hoisted out are to be drawn at 1530 and returned to the lamp room by 0800 daily for trimming and refilling. Coxswains of boats are held responsible for them when not in the lamp room.

Towing Painters.—A laden boat is always to be towed by a painter tended at both ends. Painters are to be marked with red bunting at 2 fathoms from the stem to ensure even spacing with a line of boats in tow.

Under Sail.—When under sail boats' crews are normally to get on the bottom boards. On no account should a man be allowed to stand on the thwarts.

25. UPKEEP OF BOATS

Boat Cleaners.—Two boat cleaners for each double-banked boat and one boat cleaner for each single-banked boat are to work about their boats before breakfast and at other times when asked for by the Boat Officer. They are detailed by part of ship.

Boats to be Hoisted Square.—Midshipman, or in his absence the coxswain of a boat, is responsible that a boat is square when hoisted at the davits.

Cleaning Boats after Hoisting.—Whenever a boat is hoisted in, the water-line and bottom are to be cleaned *at the time* by the appropriate boat cleaners, if on board; otherwise by members of the crew belonging to the watch on board. The coxswain of the boat or senior rating of the crew on board is responsible that this is carried out.

Oiling Boats—Care of Ship's Side.—Steamboats are not to be oiled until a screen is rigged over the side. The Midshipman (or coxswain) of the boat is responsible for the placing and returning of screen.

Power Boats' Crews.—Crews of power boats having two crews will, when running, work 24 hours on and 24 hours off. Crews will relieve at 1230 daily. The duty crews will fall in with the hands at 0600 and scrub their boats out.

Non-duty crews will work as follows:

(*a*) Lie in in the morning.

(*b*) Attend Divisions and work part of ship during forenoons.

(*c*) Stand off in the afternoon but attend Evening Quarters.

(*d*) Be allowed Watch-keepers' Leave from 1300. When at sea, Power Boats' Crews will work in with the hands, except that the duty power boats' crews on the night previous to the ship leaving harbour will make and mend clothes on the following afternoon.

26. QUARTERMASTERS, BOATSWAIN'S MATES, SIDE-BOYS AND CALL-BOYS

(1) *Quartermasters.*—Work in four watches, both in harbour and at sea, under the orders of the O.O.W.

(2) *Boatswain's Mates:*

    (*a*) *Harbour.* P.O. B.M. keeps watch on Midship Gangway.
                A.B. B.M.   "   "   with Q.M. on Q.D.

    (*b*) *At Sea.*   P.O B.M. keeps watch in four watches under orders of O.O.W., at Fore end of Boat Deck.
                A.B. B.M. keeps watch on Q.D.

(3) *Side-boys and Call-boys.*—Arranged by Boys' Instructor:

    (*a*) *Harbour.* On Q.D.   2 Side-boys.
              "   "   1 Call-boy.
              "   "   1 Messenger.
          Mid-ship Gangway.   2 Call-boys.

    (*b*) *At Sea.*   On Q.D.   1 Call-boy.
          Fore Shelter Deck.   2 Call-boys.

27. PIPING

(1) *Responsibility.*—Chief Boatswain's Mate. Is responsible that Q.M.'s and Boatswain's Mates are proficient in piping and passing calls.

Officer of Boys' Division. Is responsible that Call-boys are proficient.

(2) *Correct Method.*—The correct method of using a Boatswain's Call is laid down in 'Manual of Seamanship,' Vol. 1 (1932), p. 426, and the ship's company should be able to detect from the length and variations of a pipe what is afoot.

(3) *Orders.*—O.O.W. is responsible that ratings on watch use the Boatswain's Call correctly and effectively, and that the pipe is followed by a loud, clear order.

(4) *Piping Party.*—The Piping Party will be used for inspections and special occasions and will consist of the following:

    Commd. Boatswain.   All Q.M.'s.
    Chief Boatswain's Mate.   4 Boatswain's Mates (P.O.).
    Chief Q.M.   4   "   "   (A.B.).

The Piping Party is to be exercised as necessary under the orders of the Commd. Boatswain.

28. PIPING AND ROUTES FOR PIPING

(1) *General.*

(*a*) Before 0730 there is to be no Piping or Bugling on the Quarterdeck forward of the after hatch to Cabin Flat, or in the Batteries abaft S.6 or P.6 5.5-in. guns.

(b) When the Watch of the Hands or Both Watches of the Hands are required during working hours, the O.O.W. in harbour or the Midshipman of the Watch aft at sea is to inform the Torpedo Office, Daylight Workshop and T.S. by telephone. He is also to pass the word to all turrets.

(2) *Harbour.*

(a) Quartermaster.—The Quartermaster is to pipe at the fore end of the Quarterdeck.

(b) A.B. Boatswain's Mate.—Pipes laid down in paragraph 5 will be piped on the following route: Outside Gunroom, through the Captain's Lobby, and outside door leading to Office Flat, down ladder and aft to outside Warrant Officers' Mess, aft in each Flat, then forward Port side to Midshipmen's Chest Flat and back to the Quarterdeck.

(c) No. 1 Quarterdeck Call-boy.—Starboard side of Messdecks to P.O.'s Mess, down to Boys' Messdeck, Starboard side, Stokers' Messdeck, aft on Main deck, W.O.'s Flat, right aft to Midshipmen's Study and up to Quarterdeck.

(d) No. 2 Quarterdeck Call-boy.—Port side of Messdecks to Heads, down to Boys' Messdeck, Stokers' Messdeck, Port side aft on Main deck, W.O.'s Flat and up to Quarterdeck.

(e) No. 1 Midship Call-boy.—Start outside Commander's Cabin, forward through Starboard Battery, Starboard side of F.X., down Head hatch and then return.

(f) No. 2 Midship Call-boy.—Start outside Wardroom Port side, along Port Battery up to Reading Room (in silent hours only), down again on to F.X., down Head hatch and then return.

(g) After 2200.—Piping on F.X. deck, including Reading Room, is done by P.O. Boatswain's Mate. Piping on Messdecks by A.B. Boatswain's Mate.

(3) *At Sea.* (If Pipe is originated from Aft.)

(a) A.B. Boatswain's Mate.—Pipes laid down in paragraph 5 will be piped on the following route: Outside Gunroom, through the Captain's Lobby, and outside door leading to Office Flat, down ladder and aft to outside W.O.'s Mess, aft in each Flat, then forward Port side to Midshipmen's Chest Flat and back to the Quarterdeck.

(b) No. 1 Quarterdeck Call-boy.—Port Battery, pass the word to P.O. Boatswain's Mate, then through by Daylight Workshop to Starboard Battery and return to Quarterdeck.

(c) No. 2 Quarterdeck Call-boy.—Port side of Messdecks to Heads, down to Boys' and Fore Lower Messdecks, up to P.O.'s Mess and aft Starboard side.

(d) P.O. Boatswain's Mate.—Pipes only at his post.

(e) No. 1 Call-boy Forward.—Port side of Boat deck, Reading Room (in silent hours), Port side of F.X. and down Sick Bay Flat hatch.

(*f*) No. 2 Call-boy Forward.—Starboard side of Boat deck, Starboard side of F.X. and down Head Flat hatch.

(*3a*) *At Sea.* (If Pipe is originated from Forward.)

(*a*) P.O. Boatswain's Mate.—Gives Pipe to the two Forward Call-boys, pipes himself at his post, and informs Mid. O.W. aft or A.B. Boatswain's Mate by telephone.

(*b*) No. 1 Call-boy Forward.—Port side of Boat deck, Reading Room (in silent hours), Port side of F.X. and down Sick Bay Flat hatch.

(*c*) No. 2 Call-boy Forward.—Starboard side of Boat deck, Starboard side of F.X. and down Head Flat hatch.

(*d*) A.B. Boatswain's Mate.—Pipes laid down in paragraph 5 will be piped on the following route: Outside Gunroom, through the Captain's Lobby, and outside door leading to Office Flat, down ladder and aft to outside W.O.'s Mess, aft in each Flat, then forward to Port side in Midshipmen's Chest Flat and back to Quarterdeck.

(*e*) No. 1 Quarterdeck Call-boy.—Port Battery, pass the word to P.O. Boatswain's Mate, then through by Daylight Workshop to Starboard Battery and return to Quarterdeck.

(*f*) No. 2 Quarterdeck Call-boy.—Port side of Messdecks to Heads, down to Boys' and Fore Lower Messdecks, up to P.O.'s Mess and aft Starboard side.

(4) *Leave Periods.*

When the number of Boatswain's Mates and Call-boys is reduced, the routes are to be covered as far as possible by the ratings available.

(5) *Routine Times for Pipes, Able Seamen Boatswain's Mates.*

Daily Harbour Routine

0700.	Hands to breakfast and clean.
0750.	Out Pipes.
0830.	Both Watches of the Hands.
0905.	Divisions.
1030.	Stand easy.
1040.	Out Pipes.
1115.	Up spirits.
1130.	Afternoon watchmen to dinner.
1150.	Secure.
1200.	Dinner.
1310.	Out Pipes.
1315.	Both Watches of the Hands.
1420.	Stand easy.
1430.	Out Pipes.
1530.	First Dog Watchmen to tea.
1540.	Secure. Off overalls.
1600.	Evening Quarters.
1700.	Engine Room Department Evening Quarters.

Saturday Routine

0700.	Hands to breakfast and clean.
0750.	Out Pipes.
0755.	Both Watches of the Hands.
1030.	Stand easy.
1040.	Quarters clean guns.
1120.	Both watches clear up decks.
1150.	Secure.
1200.	Dinner.

Sunday Routine (Harbour)

0700.	Hands to breakfast.
0750.	Out Pipes.
0820.	Both Watches of the Hands.
0910.	Hands to clean.
0930.	Divisions.
——	Divine Service.
1540.	Remainder of both Watches of the Hands clear up decks.
1600.	Evening Quarters.

Make and Mend Clothes

1535.	Out Pipes.
1540.	Both Watches of the Hands.
1600.	Evening Quarters.

Sea Routine

As for Daily Harbour Routine.

Liberty Boats and Recreation Parties.

In addition to the above Pipes, the *Main* Liberty Boats each day are to be piped aft, and also *All* Pipes affecting Recreation Parties.

Note.—The above times and Pipes are always to be adhered to. If any other Pipes are required to be piped aft, they will be done by order of the O.O.W. or Midshipman of the Watch aft at sea.

29. DUTIES OF BUGLERS

(1) *Watch-keeping.*

From 0525 to 2105, one bugler will keep watch on the Quarterdeck under the O.O.W.

A second bugler is to be on duty in the Starboard Battery under the Boatswain's Mate from 0815 to 1600 (1200 on Make-and-Mend Days).

The second bugler repeats at once in the Starboard Battery all bugle calls from the Q.D.

(2) *Routes for Buglers in Harbour.*

Quarterdeck Bugler (positions marked with a brass letter 'B').

(*a*) Sounds off Starboard side of Quarterdeck (except at 0600, when he sounds off in Starboard Battery).

(*b*) At entrance to Marines' Messdeck.

(*c*) Across passage to Quarterdeck Messdeck.

(*d*) Returns across passage and forward Starboard side, to a point between Top and Forecastle Messdecks.

(*e*) Outside Petty Officers' Mess.

(*f*) Down hatch and to a point between Boys' Messdecks. Then returns to Upper deck, and to the Quarterdeck.

(2a) *Routes for Buglers at Sea.*

Fore Bugler.—Will sound off at fore end of Boat deck both sides, then down to Starboard Battery, then as for Harbour Battery Bugler.

After Bugler (positions marked with a brass letter 'B').

(*a*) Sounds off Starboard side of Quarterdeck (except at 0600, when he sounds off in Starboard Battery).

(*b*) At entrance to Marines' Messdeck.

(*c*) Across passage to Quarterdeck Messdeck.

(*d*) Returns across passage and forward Starboard side, to a point between Top and Forecastle Messdecks.

(*e*) Outside Petty Officers' Mess.

(*f*) Down hatch, and to a point between Young Seamen's and Boys' Messdecks.

Then returns to Upper deck and to the Quarterdeck.

Harbour Battery Bugler.

(*a*) Repeats Quarterdeck call in Starboard Battery.

(*b*) Forward to Starboard Embrasure.

(c) Abreast 'A' and 'B' Turrets.

(*d*) Down Head Flat.

(*e*) Aft, on Forecastle Port side, to Port Embrasure.

(*f*) Port Battery.

Then returns to Starboard Battery.

Notes.

    (i) 'G' at 1305 and 'Out Pipes' at 1310 is to be sounded at foot of Officers' after hatch between (*a*) and (*b*) in Routes for Buglers in Harbour.

    (ii) Buglers, during Forenoon and Afternoon Watches, when not in No. 1's, can be employed cleaning Drums and B and Gear in the Captain's Lobby.

(3) *Massed Buglers will sound:*

(*a*) Sundays.—Massed Buglers will sound off Officer's call at 0925 with Band and 0930 'Divisions.'

'Divisions' and 'Evening Quarters' at after end of Starboard Battery, facing forward, on Sundays and weekdays.

(*b*) *Colours.*—R.M. Buglers with Band.

Seamen Buglers are to be stationed at after end and one at the foremost end of the lee side of the Boat deck, facing forward. They will sound off the 'Attention' with signal from the Bridge and the 'Carry on' in succession from the Quarterdeck.

Note.—Seamen Buglers relieve R.M. Buglers on watch at 0730.

(c) *Sunset.*—All Buglers on board are to be stationed on after end of Boat deck, except one who is to be at the foremost end as for 'Colours,' sounding off the 'Attention' and the 'Carry on' only.

(d) *Method of Sounding.*—All calls are to be sounded off at the Halt and are never to be hurried.

(4) *Entering and Leaving Harbour.*

All Royal Marine Buglers will be massed on 'X' Turret.

All Seamen Buglers will be massed on 'B' Turret.

(5) *Sergeant of Guard.*

Will be in charge of Buglers, regulating their Watches, and will be responsible for the above Orders being carried out.

30. BUGLE CALLS

(1) *The following Bugle Calls will be used with their direct meaning:*

'Advance.'	'Commence.'	'Guard.'
'Alert.'	'Cooks.'	'Halt.'
'Attention.'	'Defaulters.'	'Lime Juice.'
'Band.'	'Disperse.'	'March at Ease.'
'Buglers.'	'Double.'	'Quick.'
'Carry on.'	'Extend.'	'Retire.'
'Cease Firing.'	'Grog.'	'Still.'
'Close.'		

(2) *The following meanings will attach to the Bugle Calls shown below:*

Meaning	Bugle Call	Remarks
Action Stations .	' Action ' 1 G — 1 G ' Action ' and 2 G's 2 G's — 2 G's	Day Action in War only Daytime for Exercise Night Action in War only ,, ,, for Exercise
Action—lull in .	' Extend '	
Action—about to cease	' Close '	
Belay . . .	' Halt '	To annul a pipe or bugle call
Buglers—Ship's .	' Buglers '	2 Seamen and 2 Royal Marines
Buglers—All . .	' Buglers ' — 2 G's	All Buglers in the ship, including volunteer bugler
Cable Party . .	' Advance ' — 1 G — 2 G's	Cable Party of Both Watches ,, ,, ,, Starb. Watch ,, ,, ,, Port ,,
Captain's Defaulters	' Defaulters ' 1 G	Captain's Defaulters and Request-men

Meaning	Bugle Call	Remarks
Clean Guns . .	' Clean Guns ' — 1 G	Normal Cleaning Stations Clean Arms
Clear Lower Deck .	' Charge ' (Dismounted) followed by ' Close '	Clear Lower Deck Clear Lower Deck—Everybody Aft
Close all W.T. Doors	Succession of short ' G's '	Close all doors as laid down in Ship's Organisation
Control Party .	1st Part of ' Sunset ' —— 1 G —— 2 G's —— 3 G's 1 G —— 2 G's ——	All Control Parties 15-inch Control Parties 5.5 ,, ,, ,, H.A. ,, ,, ,, Action Searchlight Crews Torpedo Control and Plotting Parties
Cover Guns . .	1st Part of ' Clean Guns ' 1 G ,, ,, ,, ,, 2 G's	Uncover Guns
Cruising Stations .	1 G ' Cruising Stations ' 1 G 2 G's —— 1 G 1 G —— 2 G's 2 G's —— 2 G's	1st Part of Starboard Watch 2nd ,, ,, ,, 1st ,, Port ,, 2nd ,, ,, ,,
Darken Ship . .	' Military Lights Out '	
Divisions . .	' General Assembly '	
Duty Hands . .	' Fatigue '	
Evening Quarters .	' General Assembly '	
Fire Party . .	' Still—Military Fire Alarm —Carry on '	Calls Fire Party of duty part
Gas Alarm . .	' Attention ' and 1 G	
Landing Parties (Seamen)	' Landing Party ' —— 1 G —— 2 G's	Landing Party as detailed ' A ' Company ' B ' ,,
Libertymen . .	' Libertymen '	
Main Derrick .	' Parade for Picquet '	Necessary hands are piped
Officers' Call . .	' Officers' Call ' 4 G's —— 3 G's —— 2 G's —— 1 G —— No G's	All Officers All Executive Officers Cable Officers Officers attending Captain's Requestmen and Defaulters Officers Warned

30. BUGLE CALLS—*continued*

Meaning	Bugle Call	Remarks
P.V. Party . .	' Incline '	Calls P.V. Party of Watch as pi
Recorders . .	' Markers '	
Repel Aircraft .	' Alarm to Arms '	War only, all A.A. guns' crew Con. P.
	I G ———— I G	Exercise only, all A.A. guns' c and Con. P.
Saluting Guns' Crew	' Saluting Guns' Crews '	
Special Sea Dutymen	' Rear Guard '	
Watch of Hands .	' Charge Mounted '	Calls Both Watches of Hands
	———— I G	,, Starb. Watch of Hands
	———— 2 G's	,, Port Watch of Hands
	I G ———— I G	,, 1st Pt. Starb. Watch of Ha
	2 G's ———— I G	,, 2nd ,, ,, ,, ,,
	I G ———— 2 G's	,, 1st Pt. Port Watch of Ha
	2 G's ———— 2 G's	,, 2nd ,, ,, ,, ,, ,
Watch . . .	' Watch '	Calls Both Watches
	——— I G	,, Starboard Watch
	——— 2 G's	,, Port ,,
	I G ———— I G	,, 1st Part Starb. Watch
	2 G's ———— I G	,, 2nd ,, ,, ,,
	I G ——— 2 G's	,, 1st Part Port Watch
	2 G's ——— 2 G's	,, 2nd ,, ,, ,,

31 LEADING HAND OF WATCH

(1) *General.*—He will keep his watch under the general orders of the Officer of Watch, and normally in the vicinity of the forward gangway.

(2) *Investigations.*—He will take all men of Leading Rate and below, except Royal Marines, before the Officer of Watch for investigation. He will enter all particulars in the Gangway Rough Report Book, ascertaining from O.O.W. what charge should be entered and obtaining O.O.W.'s initials.

Entries in the Gangway Rough Report Book are to be communicated to the M.A.A. without delay. In all serious disciplinary cases, and whenever Chief or Petty Officers are to be taken before O.O.W., he is to send for M.A.A. or his representative to take charge of the case.

(3) *Libertymen.*—He will cause M.A.A. to be informed when Libertymen come on board. Libertymen below the rating of Petty Officer returning from leave are to be fallen in and the M.A.A.

informed. Libertymen returning after 2300 are to be searched, fallen in and reported to O.O.W.

(4) *Dutymen.*—C.P.O.'s and P.O.'s proceeding on or returning from duty will report to O.O.W. in a similar manner to when proceeding on leave. Leading rates and below proceeding on or returning from duty will be reported to O.O.W. and a record of such dutymen is to be kept in the book provided. Ratings joining are to be fallen in and M.A.A. informed.

(5) *Dutymen absent for Meals.*—A list of men who will be absent on duty from the midday meal is to be given into the Issue Room before grog is issued. If men out of the ship on duty do not return to the ship within a reasonable time, the M.A.A. is to be informed.

(6) *Washed Clothes.*—He is to take charge of all washed clothes hung up in improper places, turning them over to the Regulating Branch.

(7) *When the Hands Fall In.*—He is to attend when the hands fall in at 0600, 0830 and 1315, to obtain the names of any absentees and is then to find them and turn them over to the Captain of Top for the Officer of Divisions report.

(8) *Rounds.*—He is to go the rounds between Pipe Down and Réveillé at uncertain times, but at least once every hour, visiting messdecks, flats and infrequented places. When cells are occupied, he is to visit the cell flat and sight men under arrest. He is to report any irregularity to the O.O.W.

(9) *On Relief.*—He is to report himself to O.O.W.

(10) *At Sea.*—He is to keep his watch on the upper deck, normally in vicinity of fore end of Boat deck.

(11) *Men Missing.*—He is to report any man who cannot be found within an hour of being reported absent to the M.A.A.

(12) *Fire and Collision.*—He will give the Cell Keys to the M.A.A. to release cell prisoners.

32. CORPORAL OF GANGWAY

(1) *General.*—He will deal with all Royal Marines, as for Leading Hand of Watch, paragraphs (1), (2), (3), (4), (5), (7) and (11), acting under the Sergeant-Major.

(2) *Smuggling.*—He will examine all packages and baskets of laundry, etc., entering or leaving the ship and satisfy himself that no unauthorised articles are contained therein. No Government Stores of any description are to be taken out of the ship unless accompanied by a proper permit signed by a Commissioned Officer.

(3) *Wines and Spirits.*—When dutiable articles, such as tobacco, cigarettes, wines, spirits, beer, etc., enter or leave the ship, he is to send for the M.A.A. (or his representative), and an entry is to be made in the Gangway Wine and Spirit Book.

(4) *Parcels, Mails, etc.*—He is to send for the Mail R.P.O. when any mails, parcels, packages, etc., are received on board.

(5) *Reliefs.*—He will call all reliefs.

(6) *Tradesmen.*—He is responsible that no tradesmen are allowed to enter the ship without the authorised pass signed by M.A.A.

(7) *On Relief.*—He is to report himself to O.O.W.

(8) *At Sea—Corporal of Watch.*—He will be known as Corporal of Watch and will keep his watch on Q.D.

33. LIFEBUOYS

(1) *Both Buoys to be Dropped.*—When dropping lifebuoys at sea, and whether for 'Man Overboard' or for practice, both buoys are always to be thrown.

(2) *Signal to Drop.*—The Signal to the Lifebuoy Sentry to throw his lifebuoys will be a long ring on the lifebuoy bell. When he has thrown his lifebuoys, whether in response to a bell signal or otherwise, he is to make a report to that effect to O.O.W. by telephone.

(3) *Allocation of Lifebuoys:*

	No.	STOWAGE	ON LOAN TO	REMARKS
(a) *White*	2	QUARTERDECK	Q.D.	Stowed away at sea
	1	1st P.B.	F.X.	
	1	2nd P.B.	Q.D.	
	1	Capt.'s M.B.	F.X.	
	1	Ship's M.B.	Top	
(b) *Blue*	2	Forecastle	F.X.	
	1	1st Launch	Top	
	1	2nd Launch	Q.D.	
(c) *Grey*	1	Quarterdeck	Q.D.	(For use with aircraft in lieu of night lifebuoy)

Lifebuoys are Permanent Loan Stores and are issued on Loan to Officers of Divisions concerned.

34. SMOKING REGULATIONS

(1) Smoking is not permitted between decks, except in the Recreation Space and in the Heads, where smoking is only permitted in non-working hours.

(2) C.P.O.'s and P.O.'s have permission, however, to smoke in their Messes and in Offices (if approved by their Head of Department) in non-working hours.

(3) After the hands have fallen in, in the morning, smoking is never to commence until 'Breakfast,' 'Dinner' or 'Tea' is piped, or until the order 'Stand easy' is passed.

(4) *Watch-keepers.*—May smoke in the Watch-keepers' places from the time they are piped to a meal until they go on watch.

(5) The Starboard after end of the Boat deck is entirely reserved for the Admiral, and is known as the 'Admiral's Deck.'

(6) Smoking spaces are allocated as follows:

Wardroom Officers	. .	Starboard Lobby.
Gunroom Officers	. .	Port Lobby.
Warrant Officers	. .	Port after end of Boat deck.
C.P.S.'s and P.O.'s	. .	Port Battery.
Remainder of Ship's Company		Starboard Battery and F.X.
Watch-keepers: (a) Harbour		Forward Embrasure (outside Daylight Workshop).
(b) Sea	.	As for Harbour and lee side of F.X. abaft Fore Breakwater.

(7) The Ship's Company may also use Boat deck before the two Stump Derricks, but are not to use the Fore Shelter deck *(i.e.* before the C.B.M.'s Office).

(8) No smoking is to take place in the vicinity of Boat's Oiling Positions when in use.

35. SPITKIDS

Spitkids are provided as follows:

PART OF SHIP	NO.	POSITION
Forecastle .	6	2 each side of Forecastle.
		1 at top of hatch in S.3 Embrasure.
		1 at after end of S.3 Embrasure.
Top . .	6	1 at top of hatch outside Ship's Galley (Port and Starboard side).
		2 in each Battery—forward end.
Quarterdeck .	5	4 in Port Battery.
		1 on Boat deck, Port side aft.
Royal Marines	4	1 at top of hatch leading to Royal Marine Messdeck.
		3 in Starboard Battery.
Torpedo Party	2	2 outside Daylight Workshop Flat.
Boys . .	4	2 in P.3 Embrasure.
		2 forward end of Boat deck, Port side.

Place Spitkids is piped whenever 'Cooks' or 'Stand easy' is sounded.

Clean out and stow away Spitkids is piped whenever bugle 'Out Pipes' is sounded.

36. RULES CONCERNING DRESS

(1) *Deck.*—Men on the Upper deck are to be properly dressed with a cap on. The cap may be carried in the hand after working hours.

(2) *Divisions and Evening Quarters.*—The dress of the day is to be worn at Divisions and Evening Quarters.

(3) *Drill Days.*—On General Drill and General Quarters Days,

and on days when a general muster, such as air bedding, is taking place on deck, all men concerned are to be in the dress of the day by the time the drill or muster is due to start.

(4) *Gymnasium Shoes* are to be clean, and they may only be worn in the dog watches for recreation. They are not to be worn with blue uniform, whether night clothing or otherwise.

(5) *Night Clothing.*—Silk handkerchiefs are to be worn with night clothing, and brown canvas shoes may be worn after Evening Quarters.

(6) *Recreation Parties.*—Men remaining ashore after recreation are to take the proper rig for Libertymen with them and shift directly the game is over. Men returning on board are to come down to the pier and catch the first boat off.

(7) *Requestmen and Defaulters.*—Captain's Requestmen and Defaulters are to be in the dress of the day.

Commander's Defaulters are to be in the dress of the day.

(8) *Seamen's Knives.*—Knives are always to be worn by all seamen ratings.

(9) *Transfer of Kit.*—In all authorised transfer of kit, the clothes are to be taken to the M.A.A.'s Office and there marked 'D.C.' with special type, the name of the previous owner being ruled through.

37. OVERALL SUITS

(1) *Seamen working in Part of Ship.*—Are to be in the dress of day unless the ship is out of routine. Captains of Tops have authority to send men away to pull on overall suits for any work liable to damage their serge suits. This authority is given also to Coxswains of Boats on the Booms, and to those in charge of Standing Parties working on the Upper deck.

(2) *Seamen working in Standing Parties* between decks may wear overall suits at their work.

(3) *Working Parties.*—Orders will be given from the Commander's Office regarding the dress for working parties. Overall suits will be ordered when the nature of the work renders it necessary.

(4) *Breakfast and Dinner Hours.*—All men authorised to wear overall suits may wear them on the Upper deck in the breakfast and dinner hours for smoking before work.

(5) *After Working Hours.*—No one in the ship is allowed to keep on an overall suit once work is finished, unless he is actually on duty, or unless he is a watch-keeper and on watch.

(6) *Clean Overalls.*—Clean overalls are to be put on every Monday, and all overall suits are to be kept in good repair.

38. REGULATING STAFF

(1) M.A.A. allocates duties among R.P.O.'s.

(2) M.A.A. is to have books and papers ready for Commander's signature at 0815.

(3) Entering or Leaving Harbour: M.A.A. stations R.P.O.'s to see no one goes on Upper deck out of rig of day, that all scuttles are kept closed, and that no one is looking out of a scuttle, close to the glass.

(4) All R.P.O.'s on board are to attend when liberty boats are returning.

(5) They are to clear Reading Room and outlying spaces at 'Clear Lower Deck,' and when 'Both Watches of Hands' is sounded at other than routine times.

(6) M.A.A. is to keep special type for transfer of kit (see Article 36 (9)).

Duty R.P.O.—The particular duties to be performed by Duty R.P.O. are:

- (*a*) Daily Rounds, twice in forenoon, afternoon and dog watches (combined).
- (*b*) Attend at Grog Tub.
- (*c*) Dinner Rounds when ordered.
- (*d*) Attend libertymen going ashore.
- (*e*) Muster men under punishment.
- (*f*) Rounds at 2100 (or 2030) in absence of M.A.A.
- (*g*) Lights out in Messes.
- (*h*) Pipe Down.

39. DISCIPLINARY PETTY OFFICER AND PETTY OFFICER OF THE DAY

Disciplinary Petty Officer.—This duty is performed in turn by all non-watch-keeping executive P.O.'s. A roster is kept by the M.A.A. If the men under punishment consist entirely of E.R. ratings, the duty of Disciplinary P.O. will be taken by a Stoker P.O.

The duties of Disciplinary P.O. are:

(*a*) He will take charge of the men under punishment whenever they fall in, and will report them present to the O.O.W., and at Rounds at 2100.

(*b*) Having obtained the previous approval of the O.O.W. for the work proposed, he will detail men under punishment for their extra work and will supervise them in carrying it out.

(*c*) He will take them at 'extra drill' as ordered in 'Routine for Men under Punishment.'

(*d*) He will be available to assist the Regulating Branch as required.

Petty Officer of the Day.—The duty of P.O. of the Day, in accordance with K.R. and A.I., Article 1865, is to be taken in rotation by all P.O.'s of the Seamen, Stoker and Artisan branches, and by Non-Commissioned Officers of the Royal Marines, except watch-keepers, the roster being kept by M.A.A.

40. ROUTINE FOR MEN UNDER PUNISHMENT

No. 11 *Punishment.*

0505.   Call men under punishment (and Disciplinary Petty Officer).
0515.   Men under punishment muster with hammocks. Fall in half an hour before hands fall in, rig and start hoses, sweep out Reading Room, etc., as requisite.
0655.   Fall in and muster (stokers will not fall in).
1155.   Fall in and muster.
1230.   (Ordinary weekdays.) Fall in. Work as detailed until 1310.
1300.   (Make-and-Mend days.) Fall in. Work as detailed until 1540.
1700.   (Or half-hour after piping tea, if later.) One hour's rifle drill with pack. Then extra work until 1900.
2000.   Fall in and muster.
2025.   (At sea.) Fall in and reported at Rounds.
2055.   Fall in and reported at Rounds.

Note.—Any man having night duty will fall out at 2000.

(1) On all occasions of falling in, men under punishment are to be mustered by Duty R.P.O. and turned over to the Disciplinary P.O. and reported to the O.O.W.

(2) At Night Rounds men under punishment will fall in outside the M.A.A.'s Office and be reported present to the officer going the rounds.

(3) *All* men under punishment will work on the Upper deck until 'Hands fall in,' and will do one hour's rifle drill with pack from 1700 to 1800, Marines doing the latter under their own N.C.O.'s. At other times Stokers and Marines are to be turned over to their own departments.

(4) The punishment of men keeping a night watch will not commence before 'Call the hands' and will terminate at 2000.

(5) Men undergoing more than 7 days No. 11 will be allowed an evening off to wash clothes every seventh day.

No. 16 *Punishment.*—Men undergoing No. 16 Punishment will muster at 1700 and be detailed as requisite for extra work.

Mustering for Night Rounds.—Any man undergoing Nos. 8, 12 and 13 will muster with No. 11 men at 2055 (or 2025 at sea) and be reported present to the officer going the rounds.

41. NIGHT ROUNDS

(1) Night Rounds will take place at 2100 in harbour and at 2030 at sea.

(2) The following Rounds will take place:

(*a*) Commander (or Commanding Officer), and
(*b*) Duty Lieutenant-Commander (or Stand-by Officer).

(3) These Rounds are to be attended by:

    (a) Commander (or Commanding Officer).
          W.O. of Day.
          Midshipman of Watch.
          M.A.A.
          Sergeant-Major.
          Bugler.

    (b) Duty Lieutenant-Commander (or Stand-by Officer).
          Midshipman of Last Dog Watch.
          Duty R.P.O.
          Bugler (or Boatswain's Mate).

(4) Rounds will start and finish in Starboard Lobby.

(5) Midshipman of Watch reports to officers concerned '5 minutes to Rounds.'

(6) Messdecks and Flats need not be clear of men. Men are to stand to attention when 'G' is sounded on their Messdeck until Rounds have passed.

(7) The following are to stand Rounds and report as shown:

RATING	PLACE	REPORT
Duty P.O. of Division	Division's Messdeck and Spaces	'Messdecks correct. Hammock nettings restowed'
Captain of Heads	Heads	'Heads cleared up'
Duty Boys' Instr.	Boys' Messdeck	'Messdeck correct. Boys turned in'
Duty Cook Rating	Galley	'Galley fires out'
Sergeant-Major	On compn. of rounds	'Keys correct'
Duty Gunner's Mate	Mag. Keyboard	'Mag. Keys and Mag. correct'
Disciplinary P.O.	M.A.A.'s Office	'Men under punishment correct'

42. ISSUE OF SPIRITS

(1) The W.O. of the Day is to superintend the issue of spirits. He is to draw and return the key himself, and is to be present the whole time the spirit-room is open. He will be responsible that the rum is issued and mixed in accordance with K.R. and A.I., Article 1827, and that the proper persons are in attendance.

(2) Any spirit ration remaining over after all messes have received their allowance is to be poured overboard in the superintending officer's presence.

(3) The spirit ration of the men whose rum is 'stopped,' owing to their being out of the ship during the dinner hour, is to be put into a jar provided for that purpose and placed under the sentry's charge.

43. WATER—SUPPLY OF FRESH AND SALT

(1) *Pump Party.*—The E.R. Department have a standing Pump Party who look after and work:

    (a) Salt Water Pumps for all services, *i.e.* Fire Main, Wash Decks, Sanitary Services, etc.

(b) Fresh Water Pumps for all F.W. Services, *i.e.* Baths, Galleys, Drinking Tanks, etc.

(2) *Salt Water.*—Pressure is normally maintained in the Fire Main, but if large quantities of water are required, or increased pressure is necessary, the Engine Room must be informed through the Engineer's Office.

Additional pumps are always run at routine times for washing decks without special orders.

(3) *Fresh Water.*—The ship can distil sufficient water to permit a maximum daily consumption of 70 tons for drinking, washing, etc., in addition to making up lost Boiler Water, etc.

This means that when away from shore water supply, very considerable economy must be exercised in the consumption of water.

44. BATHROOMS

Routine for opening Bathrooms:

(1) The Chief and Petty Officers' Bathroom will be kept open except for half an hour before 'Night Rounds,' for clearing up. They are to be closed for inspection at 'Divisions,' 'Evening Quarters,' and 'Night Rounds.'

(2) Seamen and Marines are available as follows:

1140–1300.

1300–1400. (Watch-keepers only.)

1540–1555. (Men cleaning out of overalls for 'Evening Quarters.')

After 'Evening Quarters' until half an hour before 'Night Rounds.'

After 'Night Rounds' until 0830.

(3) *Watch-keepers.*—Watch-keepers using the bathrooms between 1300 and 1400 are to clear them up before leaving.

(4) *Economy of Water.*—Owing to the size of the ship's company, *strict economy* is necessary in the amount of water used by each person.

(5) *Disposal of Bath Water.*—Water in which men have bathed is *never* to be used for scrubbing messdecks. Nothing is to be emptied in the bathrooms except the water men have bathed in.

(6) *Towels and Washed Clothes.*—Towels or washed clothes are *not* to be hung in the bathrooms. Towels or clothes left in the bathrooms will be placed in the scran bag.

(7) *Ejectors.*—Ejectors are to be worked to free the bathrooms of water and then closed. If they are left open constantly there will be insufficient pressure to work them efficiently.

(8) *Notes for Sweepers.*—Attention is called to the orders *re* ejectors. All leakages of taps or other defects are to be reported as soon as they occur. The drain sumps are to be cleared out every day.

45. DRYING ROOM

(1) The Drying Room is opened as follows:

0700–0720.	Chief and P.O.'s only	See
0720–0740.		paragraph
1045–1130.	Chief and P.O.'s only	(9).
1230–1300.		
1700–1900.		
1900–1930.	Chief and P.O.'s only.	
2000–2015.		
2015–2045.	Chief and P.O.'s only.	

(2) The Drying Room is locked by 2045.

(3) Clothes and towels are to be clearly *marked* before being taken to the Drying Room, and sweepers are not to receive unmarked clothing or towels.

(4) No rating is to *enter* the Drying Room.

(5) The Drying Room sweeper will be present at all routine times as laid down above for the Drying Room to be open, to receive wet clothes or deliver dry ones.

(6) Every rating bringing clothes to be dried receives a chit from the sweeper marked with clothes received and the number of the rack on which they are placed. This chit must be produced to reclaim the gear when dried.

(7) When Drying Room sweeper is turn for leave ashore, a relief is to be detailed from duty part of Topmen, from 1600 (1230 Make-and-Mend days) to 2045.

The Drying Room sweeper is excused Quarters Clean Guns.

(8) One of the Duty Hands will assist the Drying Room sweeper between 1740 and 1830 daily. This Duty Hand is to be excused from Beef Party.

(9) These times are for the removal of dry clothes. Wet clothes are not to be brought.

46. KEYS

(1) Only those persons authorised to do so on the list held by the Keyboard Sentry are allowed to draw keys.

(2) Keys are to be returned to the keyboard immediately the object for which they were drawn is completed.

(3) New keys are only to be made under the direction of the Shipwright Officer. Any duplicate keys which may be discovered at any time are to be returned to the Shipwright Officer.

(4) If it should be desired to keep out until after Rounds keys which should normally be returned before that time, the person wishing to do so is to make a report to the Keyboard Sentry to this effect between quarter of an hour before Rounds and Rounds.

(5) A Key Authorisation List, giving a list of persons author-ised to draw any of the keys kept under the Sentry's charge, and a list

of keys which may be kept out after Rounds without a report being made, is issued to the Half-Deck Sentry and a copy is kept in the Commander's Office.

Poison Cupboard and Dispensary Keys

(1) The keys of the Poison Cupboard are only to be issued to a Medical Officer or, with the permission of the O.O.W., to his approved representative.

(2) When, with the O.O.W.'s permission, the key is issued to the Medical Officer's representative, the return of the key is to be reported to the O.O.W.

(3) The Dispensary is to be locked when not in use, and the Medical Officer or his representative is responsible for the safety of the key.

47. SHIP'S VISITORS
(See Captain's Standing Orders.)

(1) In general, visitors are not allowed below the Upper deck nor above the Compass Platform. Permission from the O.O.W. must be obtained for any departure from this rule.

(2) *Turrets.*—Permission for visitors to enter turrets must be obtained from the Gunnery Officer, and to visit the Engine Room from the Engineer Commander.

(3) *Positions closed to Visitors.*

Control Positions.	Conning Tower.
Director Towers.	Lower Conning Tower.
Searchlight Huts.	All W.T. Offices.
Transmitting Stations.	Torpedo Flats.

(4) Special rules will be issued as the occasion arises when large crowds are expected.

48. SHORT LEAVE ORGANISATION

(1) For the purpose of Leave, the ship's company is divided into 2 watches with 2 parts in each watch, and leave is given as piped.

(2) The following are exceptions to the foregoing rule:

(*a*) Chief Petty Officers and Petty Officers are given leave as arranged by their Heads of Departments.

(*b*) In the following departments, leave to 50 per cent. is given when leave to the watch is piped, and 25 per cent. when leave is given to the part of the watch, *and these numbers should not be exceeded except for very special reasons:*

Signal and W.T. ratings, Supply ratings, Artisans, Regulating Branch, Officers' Stewards and Cooks, Ship's Cooks and Sick Berth ratings.

(3) The following may have afternoon leave on working days,

when they can be spared by the Head of their Department, without asking special leave from the Commander:

Seamen and Stoker Writers.	Central Store Office Staff.
Officers' Stewards and Cooks.	Duty R.P.O. of previous day.
Victualling Office Staff.	Wardroom attendants.
Writers.	Postman.

(4) Except when on Long Leave, *all* ratings are to sleep on board once a week and take a turn of duty.

(5) An Executive Chief Petty Officer is always to be on board until after Quarters on Weekdays (Mondays to Fridays), until noon on Saturdays, and also for Divisions on Sundays. During leave periods, an executive C.P.O. is to be on board during normal working hours from 0800 Monday until noon on Saturday.

(6) A P.O. is always to be on board for each of the following divisions: F.X., Top, Q.D., Torpedo, Ord. Sea., Boys, Communications.

49. SHORT LEAVE ARRANGEMENTS AND LEAVE CARDS

(1) *Chief Petty Officers and Petty Officers* proceeding on short leave are to tick-off their names on the short leave board and report to the O.O.W. before leaving the ship. When they return on board they are to report to O.O.W. and cross-tick their names on their board, which will be at the Gangway.

(2) *Leading Rates and Below.*—All ratings below P.O. (including Artificers 5th Class) will fall in for inspection by O.O.W., before proceeding on leave and on returning from leave. Leading rates are to fall in in a supernumerary rank and facing the remainder.

(3) *Positions of Falling In.*—When piped to fall in, libertymen are grouped as follows:

Group I.	Seamen	. .	Starboard Battery forward.
	Marines	. .	Starboard Battery aft.
Group II.	Stokers	. .	Port Battery forward.
	Communications and		
	miscellaneous .		Port Battery aft.
Chief P.O.'s and P.O.'s		. .	Abreast Port Midship ladder.

(4) *Leave Cards.*—Every rating below the rating of P.O. is issued with a Leave Card, which is retained in his possession when on board unless he is:

(*a*) Under punishment or stoppage of leave.
(*b*) On Sick List.
(*c*) In C.D.A. Mess.

M.A.A. collects in cards of men in (*a*), (*b*) or (*c*) above, and returns their cards to them when no longer under restraint.

(5) *Information on Leave Cards.*—Ship's Book Number, Name, Rating, Non-Sub. Rating, O.N., Number of Mess, Division, Watch and Part, Home Address. Starboard Watch cards are coloured green and Port Watch cards red.

(6) *Procedure with Leave Cards.*—When libertymen are piped to fall in, their cards are handed in as follows:

Seamen . . .	to Disciplinary P.O.
Marines . . .	" Duty N.C.O.
Remainder . . .	" Duty R.P.O.

The Leave Cards are placed in special boxes, each Mess having a separate partition.

Libertymen are then reported Ready for Inspection.

(7) *Procedure with Card Boxes.*—Card Boxes are to be kept locked and in M.A.A.'s Office (except Marines).

(8) *Short Leave Books.*—Short Leave Books are to be kept as follows:

(a) One for all Chief and P.O.'s.

(b) One for Seamen ratings.

(c) One for remainder (not including Marines).

Immediately after the departure of libertymen, (b) and (c) are to be written up by the P.O.'s named in (6) above.

(9) *Libertymen returning on board.*—When libertymen return they are to be fallen in for inspection as before landing and searched, and their cards returned to them by the Disciplinary P.O. and Duty R.P.O. The latter are to draw the card boxes from the M.A.A.'s Office before libertymen arrive on board, and are to return them locked to the M.A.A.'s Office immediately cards have been handed back to the libertymen.

(10) *Turn of Leave out of Watch.*—Ratings granted a turn of leave out of watch are to hand the cards of their substitutes to the M.A.A. before leave is piped. M.A.A. is to give Disciplinary P.O. a list of all ratings granted turn of leave out of watch.

(11) *Ratings not Working in Regular Watch for Leave.*—Ratings who do not work strictly with parts of watches, *i.e.* Signallers, Telegraphists, Stewards, etc., *when on duty* are to have their cards collected by the senior ratings, who are to hand them to the M.A.A. before libertymen are piped to fall in. Cards are to be returned to these ratings after the expiration of leave.

(12) *Loss of Leave Cards.*—Ratings losing their leave cards are to report the fact immediately to the M.A.A. Ratings will normally be given 24 hours to find their cards; they are then to request to see the Commander for issue of a new card.

(13) *Alterations to Leave Cards.*—Alterations are never to be made by ratings.

50. ORDERS FOR MAILS AND POSTMAN

(1) On arrival of the ship at any port the Postman will land by the first available boat and ascertain the mail arrangements from the Post Office. He will report to the Mail Officer before landing and on return.

(2) The following are to be given a copy of the mail arrangements of the port: Commander, Secretary, Flag Captain's Secretary and Ship's Office.

(3) The Commander's Office is to be informed of any modifications required in the Boat Routine.

(4) The mail arrangements for the place, including the times of closing and arrival of the mail on board, are to be posted at each Letter Box.

(5) The Postman is personally responsible for the safe and satisfactory collecting of all letters for despatch. He is to clear the following letter boxes:

(1) Admiral.	(6) Wardroom.
(2) Secretary.	(7) Gunroom.
(3) Captain.	(8) Warrant Officers.
(4) Commander.	(9) Ship's Company.
(5) Captain's Office.	

Closing the Mail.

(6) The Postman will be responsible for putting up in good time a notice on all letter boxes stating when the mail will close. Also (on the Ship's Company Letter Box) the latest time that unstamped letters will be received in the Post Office. He will obtain both these times from the Mail Officer, who also will inform the Commander of the arrangements made.

Arrival of the Mail.

(7) On arrival of the mail on board, the Postman will sort it, assisted by the M.A.A. and R.P.O.'s. The M.A.A. and R.P.O.'s will take charge of and distribute letters to the ship's company, and the Postman all letters for officers and officers' messes. The R.P.O. for registered packets and parcels will take charge of these, and see they are delivered to their consignees and signed for in the proper book.

Late Arrivals of the Mail.

(8) 'Pipe Down' may be delayed till 2330 if it is likely that a late mail can be sorted by 2300, but the Commander or the Duty Lieutenant-Commander is to be asked permission for this.

(9) The Postman is responsible that the Mail Office is kept tidy, and that No Private Gear is stowed there and that no Unauthorised Person makes Use of the Mail Office. Smoking in the Post Office is forbidden.

(10) He is responsible to the Mail Officer that the routine ordered is carried out, and will inform him immediately of all irregularities.

51. TELEGRAMS

To ensure that telegrams are dealt with expeditiously, the following routine is to be carried out:

(1) If possible, telegrams should be collected by the Postman when he goes ashore.

When a boat is sent in for telegrams or ascertains that a telegram is awaiting collection, the Midshipman or coxswain of the boat is to collect it and stow it in his cap for safety. No other ratings are to collect and bring off a telegram unless ordered to do so.

(2) All telegrams brought off are to be handed to the O.O.W. immediately the boat returns to the ship.

(3) All telegrams are to be entered in the telegram book by the Corporal of the Gangway, and are to be delivered by him at once. The recipient is to sign the book.

(4) If the recipient is ashore, the O.O.W. will carry out the following procedure:

(a) In the case of an officer, he will open the telegram and take any necessary action. The telegram will then be placed in the recipient's letter rack, and the book initialled by O.O.W.

(b) In the case of ship's company, the telegram is to be delivered by the Corporal of the Gangway to the M.A.A. or Duty R.P.O., who will carry out the above procedure, except that the telegram is to be kept in the Police Office and delivered to the recipient on his return from shore by the M.A.A. or Duty R.P.O. personally. The M.A.A. or Duty R.P.O. will initial the book.

52. PERIODICAL CHANGE OF DUTIES

Change of duties will be worked on the following lines:

(1) Men carrying out special duties (such as Sweepers, Gunner's Party, Head Party, Messmen, etc.) will, if there is no service reason to the contrary, be given the option of changing to Part of the Ship at the end of six months.

(2) Those who prefer to stop where they are, will do another six months, when a further option will be given.

(3) Ordinary Seamen will not be allowed to do more than six months at a time in a special duty, and are then to join their Part of Ship.

(4) Able Seamen under the age of 26 will not be allowed to do more than 12 months consecutively in a special duty, and are then to join their Part of Ship.

EXECUTIVE ORGANISATION

The following routine of changes will be followed subject to the foregoing conditions:

Leading Hands.

Power Boats . .	Minimum time: 4 months.
	Maximum time: 6 months (at option).
Heads . . .	Maximum time: 6 months.

A.B.'s and Ords.

Boatswain's Party .	Two to be standing numbers (2nd period men), one to change every cruise, new-comers to be A.B.'s passed for Leading Seamen or promising Ordinary Seamen.
Men passed for Leading Seamen	To be passed through following rotation as far as possible: Part of Ship (Side Party, Gun Sweeper, Boom Sweeper, etc.), Power Boat, Part of Ship and Pulling Boat, Boatswain's Party, Part of Ship.
Special Painting Party	Three changes every cruise.
Sweepers and other duties	Above orders apply, except that men passed for Leading Seamen will do only 6 months.
Gunner's Party . .	One change every cruise.
Paymaster's Party .	One change every cruise.
Head Party . .	One change every cruise.
Side Party . .	One change every cruise, but A.B.'s passed for Leading Seamen to do only 6 months.
Double Bottom Party .	Seamen are not to serve in this party for more than 4 months.

Boys.

Change of duties is arranged by Officer of Boys' Division.

53. CINEMA RIGGING

(1) *The Cinema Rigging Party* will consist of Emergency Party:
1 Leading Seaman and 3 Torpedo.
1 N.C.O. and 3 Royal Marines.
1 Leading Stoker and 6 Stokers.

(2) *Falling In.*—On Cinema Nights, the Cinema Rigging Party will be piped to fall in in the Starboard Battery at 1830.

(3) *Duties.*

F.X. and Top .	Rig Awning Curtain.
Q.D. . .	Rig Screens on top of awning when required, or assist with Church Planks.
Torpedo, R.M. and Stokers .	Place Church Planks.

(4) *Unrigging.*—When Cinema is over, Emergency Party will be piped to 'Unrig Cinema,' and 2 hands from each Part of Ship, Marines and Stokers (10) are to be detailed to sweep up the deck.

54. LIBRARY AND BOOKSTALL

(1) The Ship's Library is kept in the School-place in the W.O.'s Flat, and is looked after by a Librarian under the direction of the Senior Master.

(2) The Bookstall, situated at the after end of the Sick Bay Flat, is managed by a Committee consisting of:

> The Commander.
> The Paymaster Commander.
> The 'Bookstall Officer.'

(3) The 'Bookstall Officer' is responsible for the general management of the Bookstall.

(4) The Bookstall is open as follows:

> Breakfast hour.
> Dinner hour.
> 1630–1830.
> 2000–2100.

(5) The profits from the Bookstall are devoted to such purposes as the Committee may recommend, subject to the Captain's approval.

55. PRIVATE TRADING

(1) *Commander's Permission* must be obtained to do Private Trading on board.

(2) *Numbers Allowed.*—Trading in the undermentioned are not to exceed the following numbers of the ship's company:

Tailors	6
Boot repairers	9
Barbers	6
Photographers	2

The M.A.A. will keep a list of men who have obtained permission to trade and a waiting list of men who wish to fill any vacancy.

(3) *Routine.*—Trading is not permitted during working hours or after Pipe Down.

(4) *Price List.*—A price list of charges approved by the Commander is to be displayed in a prominent position in the place where the trading is carried on and a duplicate list rendered to M.A.A.

(5) *Tailoring—Maximum Charges.*
(*a*) Tailor providing all material:

	s.	d.
No. 1 Suit	15	6
No. 2 "	15	0
No. 5 "	11	6
No. 6 "	13	0
Flannel	4	6

(*b*) Serge, Jean, Duck or Flannel provided by men:

	s.	d.
No. 1 Suit	7	0
No. 2 "	6	6
No. 5 "	5	0
No. 6 "	7	0
Flannel	1	6

(6) *Haircutting.*—Barbers' Shop accommodates 2 Barbers who take turn for 6 months with other barbers in ship, drawing lots. In addition there are 4 Barbers' positions as follows:
(*a*) At after end of Port Passage.
(*b*) Outside Seamen's Bathroom.
(*c*) In Boat Hoist Flat.
(*d*) Sick Bay Flat.

(7) *Barbers' Charges.*

Haircut	4*d.*
Shave	2*d.*
Self Shave	1*d.*
Wet Shampoo	4*d.*
Dry Shampoo	2*d.*
Razor Set	6*d.*

(8) *Barbers' Shop Routine.*—The shop is open as follows:
During breakfast and dinner hour.
From tea until 2130.
On Make-and-Mend afternoons.

(9) *Boys—Haircutting.*—The Barbers' Shop is reserved for boys from 1700–1800 on Thursdays and Fridays, during which times Boys' hair is cut free of charge. This privilege relieves the Barbers of any rent charges for the shop.

(10) *Boot Repairs.*

	s.	d.
Sole and heel (rivets) . . .	3	6
" " " (sewn) . . .	4	6
Soles only (rivets) . . .	2	9
" " (sewn)	3	9
Revolving rubbers . . .		7
Shaped rubbers		9

56. ROUTE FOR CAPTAIN'S SATURDAY INSPECTION

(1) *Officers' Messes, etc.*—The Captain will be met at the Starboard Lobby door on to the Q.D. by the Heads of Departments. He will then inspect the Officers' Messes and Pantries, W.O.'s first, proceeding and returning by the ladder opposite his cabin door, then the Gunroom and finally the Wardroom, and Staff Office Flat.

(2) *Divisions and Miscellaneous Inspections.*—He will then inspect the Divisions, commencing in the Commander's Lobby and going forward the Starboard side, and aft the Port side, ending on the Fore end of the Q.D. Starboard side. On this route, the following will be inspected as convenient:

5.5-in. guns, Officers' Galleys, Ship's Galley, Night Heads, Boatswain's and Gunner's R.U. Stores, Upper Deck Lockers, Drying Rooms, Bakery, Daylight Workshop, Anchors and Cables, Diving Store, F.X. Lockers, Officers' Round-houses.

(3) *Boat Deck and Bridges, etc.*—On conclusion of the above, the Captain may inspect the Boat Deck and Bridges, in which case the route will be as follows:

Up the Admiral's hatch to the Boat Deck, 4-in. guns and Q.D. Locker; forward Starboard side, inspecting Boats, Workshops and Pom-Poms on the way; up to Compass Platform, inspecting all bridges and positions. Return Port side of Boat Deck, inspecting Boats and Guns, Top Locker, Battery Room and, finally, the Sailmaker's Store.

57. ROUTE FOR INSPECTION OF STORE ROOMS

(1) On Thursday forenoons the Captain will inspect either the forward or after section of the ship below the Messdecks, *i.e.* all storerooms.

Forward Section—Stem to 133 Bulkhead.
After Section—280 Bulkhead to Stern.

The Engine Rooms and Machinery spaces will be inspected separately as convenient.

(2) The Rounds will commence at the forward end of the Section and work aft.

(3) Turrets will be inspected in turn as arranged by Lieutenant-Commander 'G.' with the Captain.

58. MISCELLANEOUS

(1) *Bathing from Ship.*—No man who has not passed the Standard Swimming Test is allowed to bathe from the ship.

(2) *Cameras.*—Captain's permission is necessary to have a camera on board. Men granted permission are to acquaint themselves with A.F.O. 1986/24.

(3) *Card-playing* is allowed until 'Pipe Down' at mess tables and in places set apart for smoking.

(4) *Complaints concerning Provisions, Cooking, Slops, etc.,* are to be made to the P.O. of the Day, who will report to the O.O.W.

(5) *Disposal of Gear found lying about.*—Any man who may find lying about articles which are not his own property is to hand them over to the M.A.A. or Duty R.P.O., who will take steps to deliver them to the proper owner. Neglect to act in this way renders a man found in possession of such articles liable to disciplinary action.

(6) *Dogs and Pet Animals* are not to be brought on board without the Commander's permission.

(7) *Fishing* may be carried out after 'Tea' is piped or on Make-and-Mend afternoons. Fishing out of scuttles or ports is not permitted. Men are to clear up the mess they make with bait, etc.

(8) *Gambling, etc.*—Gambling is forbidden. No man is to engage in any money-lending, bookmaking or betting business, either on his own account or as agent for others.

(9) *Men Absent from Meals.*—Leading Hands of Messes are to report to the M.A.A. at once, if any man is unaccountably absent from a meal.

(10) *Respirators—Anti-Gas.*—Officers of Divisions are to inspect the Anti-Gas Respirators of all ratings joining the ship within one week of arrival. They are to see that they are marked correctly. Defects are to be reported to the Anti-Gas Officer, stating official number of rating and ship from which he joined.

All ratings on draft are to carry their respirators in the slung position; on no account are they to be packed in their bags.

(11) *Ship's Side Scuttles.*—Throwing gear or water of any kind out of scuttles is forbidden. Leaning out of scuttles is forbidden, as is fishing out of scuttles.

(12) *Trafficking.*—No trafficking of any sort is allowed.

59. GENERAL MESSING

General.—The ship's company will be messed on the General Mess System, with the exception of the Officers' Messes.

Grog Money.—Grog Money will be credited on the Ledger.

Allowances.—Victualling Allowance (at present 1*s*. 1 . 2*d.*) and Allowance in lieu of Spirit (2*d.*) for men going on week-end leave are credited to the respective messes monthly.

Cooking.—All cooked dishes will be prepared by the Cookery Staff, provisions being issued to them direct.

Serving.—Cooked meals will be drawn by Cooks of Messes of the watch below from the Serving Room or Galley, when 'Cooks' is sounded.

No man other than the Cook of the watch below (or Watch-keepers) is allowed in his Mess until the meal is piped.

Dishes.—Meat dishes are to be returned to the Preparing Room by the Cook of the watch below immediately after each meal hour.

Dishes are to be thoroughly cleaned before being returned, and Cooks of Messes will be held responsible for this.

A Cook rating will be in attendance when the dishes are returned, a list of issues and returns being kept, and any shortages or cases of improperly cleaned dishes are to be reported to the Accountant Officer at once.

Menus.—Menus will be prepared weekly and posted on the notice boards, and will be adhered to as far as possible.

Extra Issues.—Extra issues (lime juice, etc.) and issue of spirits will be made as authorised by the King's Regulations.

Should a Mess desire to take up any Service provisions on repayment, the issue will be made, and will take place at the Issue Room at 1230 daily, except Saturday and Sunday.

Bread.—Bread will be issued daily from the Bakery at 1230.

Extra bread, if required, can be obtained at 0700 daily, a chit for it being given by the Cook of the Mess.

Other Issues.—Tea, sugar and milk will be issued from the Issue Room at 1230 on Fridays.

Margarine (or butter) will be issued daily from the Issue Room at 1230.

Potatoes.—Potatoes will be issued daily from the Vegetable Locker at 1230. They are to be returned to the Preparing Room between 1700 and 1900, peeled and ready for cooking in properly marked nets.

Night and Week-end Leave.—Leading Hands of Messes are to see that the following information on a chit is given to the Issue Room by the Cook of their Mess not later than the times mentioned:

(1) By 0900 each day. The number of men in the mess proceeding on night leave, so that the proper number of suppers can be prepared.

(2) By 0900 on Fridays. The number of men proceeding on week-end leave.

Private Meals are not allowed to be cooked in the Galley. Exceptions may be made in special cases, but only by permission of the Accountant Officer.

Galley, etc.—No one, other than the Cookery Staff, is allowed in the Galley, Preparing Room, Serving Room or Bakery.

Waste.—The co-operation of the ship's company in the prevention of waste will be a large factor in the success of the General Messing.

EXECUTIVE ORGANISATION

Supplies.—Supplies are obtained from outside as well as from Service sources, in order to provide variety of menu, but this can only be done if the Messing is run economically and with no waste.

Complaints.—Any mess having a complaint as regards the quantity or quality of the food served is immediately to take the whole dish back to the C.P.O. Cook in charge of the Galley, who will at once deal with the matter, referring, if necessary, to the Accountant Officer. Normally this procedure should ensure settlement of complaints, but it does not debar messes from representing a complaint to the Officer of the Watch through the P.O. of the Day, should they wish to do so after action has been taken as above.

Suggestions.—Suggestions for improving the meals will be welcomed, and Leading Hands of Messes wishing to put forward suggestions should submit them to the Accountant Officer.

60. PAYMENTS

Money will be paid fortnightly on alternate Fridays.

Payment is made simultaneously in the Port and Starboard Lobbies as follows:

Starboard Side: Seamen.

Port Side: E.R. ratings, miscellaneous ratings and Marines.

Also R.N.R. and R.N.V.R. ratings when borne.

Men are fallen in on the F.X. deck (Port and Starboard side as above) in Ship's Books Numbers, and proceed in single file past the Pay Table, and then down hatch abaft Pay Table and forward to messdecks.

Hundreds are to be controlled on the F.X. deck by their officers, and formed into single file at the entrance to the lobby.

Postal Orders can be obtained on Tuesday and Saturday at the Paymaster Lieutenant-Commander's Office between 1015 and 1030.

61. CENTRAL STORE SYSTEM

(1) All stores in the ship are obtained in the first place from the Central Store.

(2) *Permanent Stores.*—Each Officer of Division is responsible for the permanent stores, *e.g.* Hoses, Branch Pipes, gear in Bathrooms, etc., in his part of the ship. He is to be given a list of these stores, and a corresponding list, signed by him, is kept in the Central Store Office.

Replacement of defective permanent stores is carried out by returning the article to the Main Central Store with a Return Chit (S. 1091) made out in duplicate, and a Demand Note made out on Form S. 156, endorsed '*Permanent Stores.*' The duplicate of the Return Chit (S. 1091) will be signed by the Central Store Staff as a receipt.

(3) *Consumable Stores.*—Consumable stores such as cleaning gear, cordage, canvas, paint, etc., can only be drawn on the Executive Officer's account under the signature of the First Lieutenant or Officer in the Commander's Office. Stores required for repairs and refitting, etc., can be drawn under the signature of the Commd. Boatswain, Commd. Signal Boatswain and Commd. Shipwright.

(4) The Money Allowance to the Executive Department is limited, and the strictest economy is necessary to keep within it.

(5) *Cleaning Gear.*—The weekly allowance of cleaning gear is laid down by the Commander, and that allowance can be drawn weekly on Fridays by the part of the ship concerned. The rating drawing cleaning gear for the part of the ship concerned will sign in the Cleaning Gear Book kept in the Cleaning Gear Store.

Form S. 156 is to be made out in the Commander's Office, signed by the Commander or Officer in the Commander's Office, for the total quantity of cleaning gear issued each Friday. This form (S. 156) is to be sent to the Central Store Office *before* issue of cleaning gear is actually made.

(6) *Cordage and Canvas Gear.*—The Boatswain's Yeoman and Sailmaker, respectively, keep a small stock of the cordage and canvas more usually required for the smaller jobs which crop up from day to day, and the Commd. Boatswain is authorised to meet the requirements of Officers of Divisions to that extent, consulting the Officer in the Commander's Office as necessary.

(7) *Paint.*—The Commd. Shipwright is supplied with paint in bulk, and also with pots and brushes. He is responsible for the issue of the necessary paint, pots and brushes to the parties requiring it. Such requirements must be supported by a chit signed by one of the officers mentioned in paragraph 3.

(8) Except in the case of the Special Painting Party and Side Party, who are authorised to retain their paint and brushes, all pots and brushes are to be returned to the Paint Shop each day on completion of work.

If required for the next day, a chit to that effect should be attached to the brush.

(9) The Commd. Shipwright and an Officer detailed by the Commander will hold a survey every quarter and decide what brushes and tools must be replaced by new.

62. ISSUE OF CLOTHING

Clothing will be issued between 1130 and 1200 as follows:

C.P.O.'s and P.O.'s	.	Mondays.
Ship's Company	.	Tuesday to Friday.
Boys	.	Friday (being Pay Day) at 1330.

Clothing Issue Notes are to be handed in by 0900 daily.

Cash is to be paid to the Accountant Officer or his representative at the time of issue of the clothing.

Clothing issued to Boys will be charged against their accounts in the Ledger as a Casual Payment.

63. ISSUE OF SOAP AND TOBACCO

Soap and tobacco will be issued in bulk to messes on the first day of each month.

Mess lists of requirements are to be given in to the Issue Room twenty-four hours before issue. Cash is to be paid at the time of issue.

64. STANDING ISSUE OF CLEANING GEAR TO THE UPPER DECK AND MESSDECKS

Department	Soap, Hard	Soap, Soft	Soda, Common	Waste	Metal Polish	Cloth, Cleaning	Cloth, Emery	Paper, Glass	Powder, Cleansing	Izal
Messdecks .	64	56	50	14	72	10	72	—	10	4
Royal Marines	40	36	24	20	32	8	68	—	18	1
W.O.'s Mess .	2	—	9	2	2	2	2	—	2	—
Wardroom .	2	7	2	2	2	2	2	—	2	—
Gun Room .	2	7	2	2	2	2	2	—	2	—
Issue Room .	8	10	12	4	8	2	6	—	2	—
Chief Cook .	12	10	20	4	4	2	6	—	10	1
Adml.'s Galley	2	2	1	2	2	1	2	—	2	—
Adml.'s Sec.'s Office . .	2	2	—	2	2	1	2	—	2	—
Top Div. .	20	12	14	12	18	6	10	—	12	—
F.X. Div. .	12	12	14	12	18	6	10	—	12	—
Q.D. Div. .	20	12	14	12	21	6	10	—	12	—
Adml.'s Qtrs.	9	—	6	4	18	1	2	2	—	—
Captain's Qtrs.	4	3	6	1	2	2	2	—	2	—
Signal Dept. .	5	8	5	8	16	1	4	2	—	—
Chief Q.M. .	6	8	2	4	14	4	4	—	—	—
Totals .	210	185	181	105	233	56	204	4	88	6
Price per .	lb. 4d.	lb. 2d.	lb. ½d.	lb. 6d.	Tin 2d.	Yd.9d.	Sht.1d.	Sht.¼d.	1lb.1d.	G. 3/6
Total values	70/-	30/10	7/7	52/6	38/10	42/-	17/-	1d.	7/4	21/-

Total cost of weekly issue of cleaning gear : £14 7s. 2d. for upper deck and messdecks.

65. CANTEEN COMMITTEE

The Canteen Committee is formed as follows:

(1)   *Ex-Officio Members*

The Commander   .   .   .   .   President.
The First Lieutenant   .   .   .   .   Vice-President.
The Paymaster Commander   .   .   Hon. Treasurer.

| A Commissioned Officer | . | . | . | Hon. Secretary. |
| A Chief Petty Officer Writer | . | . | | Secretary. |

Elected Members		No. of Representatives
C.P.O.'s, Seamen and Daymen . .		One
C.P.O.'s, Engine Room . . .		,,
P.O.'s, Seamen and Daymen . .		,,
P.O.'s, Engine Room . . .		,,
Seamen, Forecastle Division . .		,,
Seamen, Top Division . . .		,,
Seamen, Quarterdeck Division . .		,,
Communication Branch . . .		,,
E.A.'s, O.A.'s and Shipwrights . .		,,
Daymen below Petty Officer . .		,,
Leading Stokers and Stokers . .		Two
N.C.O.'s, Royal Marines . . .		One
Royal Marines		,,

(2) *Voting.*—Each representative member has one vote and the President (or Vice-President) has a casting vote when necessary.

(3) *Meetings.*—The Committee meets on the first and third Saturday of each month during the ship's cruises, with one meeting prior to the commencement of leave periods.

(4) *Procedure.*—The following procedure is to be carried out during the week preceding the meeting:

Tuesday.—Insert in Commander's Daily Orders: 'The Canteen Committee will meet on Saturday. All items for the agenda must reach the Secretary by 0800 on Wednesday.'

Wednesday.—0800. The latest time for receiving items for the agenda.

66. MUSTERING BY OPEN LIST

The Ship's Book List is grouped as follows for Open List, Payments and Issues:

HUNDRED	LIST	COMPOSED OF	NO. OFFICER
1st	5/1	C.P.O.'s and P.O.'s (Seamen, Sigs. and Tels.)	
2nd	5/2	Seamen, Sigs. and Tels.	
3rd	5/2	Seamen, Sigs. and Tels.	
4th	5/A1	C.P.O.'s and P.O.'s (Engine Room)	
5th	5/A2	Leading Stokers, Stokers 1st class and 2nd class	

Hundred	List	Composed of	No. Officer
	5/B1	C.P.O.'s and P.O.'s (Artisan Branch)	
	5/C1	Sick Berth C.P.O. and P.O.	
	5/C2	Sick Berth Attendant	
6th	5/D1	C.P.O.'s and P.O.'s (Accountant Branch)	
	5/D2	L. Cooks and Cooks, Wtrs., S.A.'s, Off. Stds. and Cooks, 2nd class and below	
	5/E1	M.A.A. and R.P.O.'s	
	9/1	Bandmaster	
	9/2	Musicians and Band Boys	
7th	11/1	Marines (Sergeants)	
	11/2	Marines	

Attention is to be paid to the following points:

(1) Maintaining front section of fours complete, at point where single file is formed.

(2) That each man looks the Inspecting Officer (and no one else) full in the face.

(3) That each man calls out those qualifications (rating, subst. and non-subst., badges, etc.) for which he draws pay.

67. ORDERS FOR PAINTING

For Painting Ship, the whole of both watches will be employed. Other painting will be confined as much as possible to small parties of experienced men.

It is inexcusable to paint over dirt. The paintwork to be coated is first to be washed with fresh water and allowed to dry. Every man painting is to have a cloth or piece of cotton waste with which to wipe off dirt before applying paint.

The greatest care is to be taken that any paint which gets on to bright-work, glass, and especially woodwork, is wiped off immediately while it is still wet.

Later it is difficult to remove, and varnished wood is ruined.

Leading Hands of painting parties will be held answerable for this order being carried out, and are, if necessary, to tell off a proportion of their hands for this cleaning-off work only.

On the weather decks, Rust will be the chief enemy. The only cure is to scrape close round each individual rust mark, force in a little oil for two or three consecutive days (the rust soaks up this oil and is held by it), allow the spot to dry thoroughly and, lastly, paint over it again.

Engraved tally plates, on electrical boxes or elsewhere, are never to be painted over.

68. SPORTS ORGANISATION

1. *Management of Sports.*

(*a*) *Officers in Charge.*—An officer is in general charge of the management of each sport and responsible to the Commander, who is to be kept fully informed of the progress of the sport.

(*b*) *Committees of Management.*—A Committee of Management is formed for each sport. In certain cases, *e.g.* Football, the Committee is formed of representatives from each Part of Ship; in other cases, *e.g.* Cinema, representatives of each branch.

Election of Inter-Part Committee is held as necessary from time to time.

(*c*) *Lists of Committees.*—A complete list of all committees is shown on a special board in a prominent position.

(*d*) *Ship's Selection Committees* are chosen by the Committee of Management of each sport from their own members, and an asterisk will be placed against their names on the above board.

(*e*) *Qualifications for Membership of Committees.*—The essential qualifications for membership of Management or Selection Committee are:

(1) Real knowledge of the game concerned.

(2) Readiness to give time to organising and watching games.

(3) Zeal in bringing to light the requirements and abilities of those represented.

(*f*) *Meetings of Committees.*—Each Management Committee is to meet at the commencement of each cruise in which the particular sport will be indulged in, to determine policy and publish a programme, and it is subsequently to meet as required.

The Football Management Committee is to meet once a week during the football season. A brief report of meetings is to be published.

2. *Funds for Sports.*

Funds are provided by contributions from the Ship's Fund as sanctioned by the Canteen Committee. Committees of Management are to incur no expenditure involving the Ship's Fund without reference to the Canteen Committee.

3. *Publication of Sporting News* comes under three headings:

(*a*) Forthcoming fixtures.

(*b*) To-day's fixtures.

(*c*) Results.

(*a*) *Forthcoming Fixtures.*—It is essential that the Management Committee of individual sports notify the Commander's Office of all dates arranged (including provisional dates), however far ahead, as soon as they have been fixed. A forecasting diary is kept in the Commander's Office, which will assist in avoiding date clashing.

EXECUTIVE ORGANISATION

(b) *To-day's Fixtures.*—The sporting fixtures for each day will be attached to the Commander's Daily Orders in a special Daily Recreation Programme. They are to reach the Commander's Office by 1430 the previous day.

(c) *Results.*—Immediately after each game or contest, information of the result is to be given in to the Commander's Office. These results will be published in the Daily Recreation Programme.

4. *Sports Gear.*

(a) *Purchasing Gear.*—The P. and R.T. Officer will purchase the necessary sports gear with funds authorised by the Canteen Committee, giving preference to the N.A.A.F.I. in making purchases.

(b) *Charge of Gear.*—A rating will be placed in charge of the sports' gear and remunerated by the Canteen Committee for this duty and for washing and repairing the gear. This rating will be held responsible for the issue and return of the gear.

69. DAILY HARBOUR ROUTINE

(Times marked with asterisk are to be reported to Commander.)

0505. Call Ratings under Punishment and Boy Cooks.

0515. Call the Boys, Duty Petty Officers, Bugler and Emergency Party.

0525. Boys fall in with hammocks on Messdeck.

0530. Call the hands. Lash up and stow. Emergency Party fall in.

0535. Cooks to the Galley for cocoa.

0545. Hands to cocoa and wash. Duty Boys of the Morning Watch fall in.

*0550. 'G.' Boys fall in for Physical Training.

0555. Out Pipes.

*0600. Hands fall in. Clean Ship. Lower and clean out Duty Boats. Power Boats to oil and water.

0615. Up Guard and Steerage hammocks.

0625. Steerage Hammock Boys fall in.

0630. Dry down the Upper deck.

0645. Off Boat-ropes and Sternfasts. Open 'B' doors.

0650. Cooks. Uncover Guns. Respread awnings.

*0700. Hands to breakfast and clean. Pipe rig of the day.

0745. 'G.' Guard and Band call (Summer routine).

0750. Out Pipes. Duty Boys of the Forenoon Watch fall in for inspection.

0755. Quarters Clean Guns. Special parties excused Clean guns fall in.

0820. Commander's Requestmen and Defaulters.

*0825. 'G.' Return rags.

0830. Both Watches of the Hands. Clean Messdecks and Flats. Finish off the Upper deck and clean bright-work.

0845. Guard and Band call (Winter routine). Boat for Commander.

0850.	Watch-keepers Out Pipes.
*0900.	'G.' Buglers' call. Cooks fall in when there are no Divisions.
0905.	Divisions. Prayers. Physical Drill, etc. Then: Both Watches.
*1030.	Stand easy.
1040.	Out Pipes. Hands carry on with work.
*1115.	Up spirits.
1130.	Afternoon Watchmen and relief boats' crews to dinner.
1140.	Clear up decks.
*1150.	Secure. Cooks. Grog.
*1200.	Dinner. Pipe leave.
1220.	Duty Boys of Afternoon Watch fall in for inspection.
1305.	'G.'
*1310.	Out Pipes.
*1315.	Both Watches of Hands fall in.
*1420.	Stand easy.
1430.	Hands carry on with work.
1530.	First Dog Watchmen to tea.
*1545.	Secure. Take off overalls. Both Watches fall in. Clear up decks.
1550.	Duty Boys of the first Dog Watch fall in for inspection.
1555.	Buglers' call.
*1600.	Evening Quarters. Then: Cooks. Tea. Hands shift into night clothing. Libertymen to clean.
1645.	Libertymen fall in.
1700.	Engine Room Department to Evening Quarters. Duty hands fall in. Up fresh provisions.
1750.	Duty Boys of the last Dog Watch fall in for inspection.
1800.	Libertymen fall in.
1900.	Supper. Duty Boats' crews shift into night clothing.
1945.	Officers' Dress Call. Boys stand by hammocks.
2000.	Officers' Dinner Call. Stand by hammocks.
*2030.	Cooks and Sweepers clear up Messdecks and Flats. Remainder of the Duty Part of Watch of Hands fall in. Stand fast Torpedo Party. Sweep down Upper deck. Place Scrub Deck Gear. Close 'B' and 'C' doors. Slope awnings.
2045.	First Post. Boys turn in.
2050.	Emergency Party fall in with oilskins.
*2100.	Rounds. Last Post.
2200.	Pipe Down.
2230.	Chief and Petty Officers Pipe Down.

70. ROUTINE FOR MAKING AND MENDING CLOTHES

1530. 'G.'
1535. Out Pipes.
1540. Both Watches of Hands. (Clear up decks. Cooks and Sweepers clear up messdecks.)
1555. Buglers' call.

Then as for 'Daily Harbour Routine.'

71. SEA ROUTINE

Note.—Normally, the Duty Part of the Watch will be the Watch on Deck.

As for 'Daily Harbour Routine,' except as follows:

0345. Call the Morning Watch.
0355. Morning Watch to muster.
0515. Morning Watch to muster. (Place Wash Deck Gear and sweep down the Upper deck.) Call R.P.O. and Bugler.
0540. Morning Watchmen fall out. Hands to cocoa and wash.
0700. Sea-boat's Crew of Morning Watch to muster.
0755. Sea-boat's Crew of Morning and Forenoon Watches to muster and relieve. Morning Watch Crew to breakfast.
0900. Morning Watch Sea-boat's Crew fall in.
1130. Sea-boat's Crew and First Trick of Afternoon Watchmen to dinner.
1225. Sea-boat's Crew of Afternoon Watch to muster.
1315. Middle Watchmen, Sea-boat's Crew of Forenoon Watch and Last Tricks of Forenoon Watch stand fast from Both Watches of Hands fall in. Both Watches of Hands fall in.
1345. Sea-boat's Crew and Last Trick of Forenoon Watch fall in.
*1530. Sea-boat's Crew and First Trick of Dog Watchmen to tea. At Evening Quarters: First Dog Watchmen and Sea-boat's Crews of Afternoon and First Dog Watch to muster and relieve after disperse.
1700. Duty Hands fall in. Up fresh provisions.
1755. Last Dog Watchmen and Sea-boat's Crew to muster.
1945. Stand by hammocks.
1955. First Watchmen and Sea-boat's Crew to muster. Clear up Messdecks and Flats for Rounds.
*2030. Night Rounds.
2125. Out Pipes.
2130. Pipe Down. First Watch to muster.
2345. Call Middle Watch.
2355. Middle Watch to muster.

72. SATURDAY ROUTINE

Daily Routine, except as follows:

  Upper deck not to be dried down before breakfast.

  No Guard and Band.

0755.   Both Watches of Hands fall in. Clean Messdecks and Flats. Finish off Upper deck. Uncover Guns after the Hands have been detailed.

1000.   'G.' Up all Deck Cloths on Messdecks and Flats.

1010.   Stand easy.

1015.   Band call.

1020.   Out Pipes. Quarters Clean Guns. Captain's Rounds of the Messdecks and Flats.

1045.   'G.' Return rags. Up spirits.

1050.   Both Watches fall in. Clear up decks for Divisions.

1100.   Up all Upper deck Deck Cloths.

1110.   Hands to clean into No. i's. Band call and buglers.

1120.   Officers' Call—4 G's.

1125.   Divisions. Fall in as for Sunday Divisions. Captain's Inspection of Divisions, Upper deck, Boat deck and Bridges.

1130.   Afternoon Watchmen to dinner.

1155.   Disperse. Cooks. Grog.

1200.   Dinner. Pipe leave.

  Hands to Make-and-Mend clothes.

    Then as for 'Daily Harbour Routine.'

  Note.—On the day selected by the Captain for his Weekly Inspection of Messdecks, Cooks remain below until 1030, and Messdeck Rounds are commenced at 1040.

73. SUNDAY ROUTINE

'A'—*Harbour*

0600.   Réveillé.

0615.   Up Guard and Steerage hammocks.

0650.   Cooks.

0700.   Breakfast.

0735.   'G.'

0740.   Out Pipes.

0745.   Quarters Clean Guns.

0805.   'G.' Return rags.

0810.   Both Watches of Hands fall in. Clean Messdecks and Flats. Remainder clear up decks and clean bright-work.

0910.   Hands to clean.

0930.   Clear off the Messdecks and Flats. Hands carry on smoking.

0940.   Pipe Down.

0945.   Church.

1115. Up spirits.
1130. Afternoon Watchmen to dinner.
1150. Cooks. Grog.
1200. Dinner. Pipe leave.

Then as for 'Make-and-Mend Routine.'

'B'—Sea

As for 'A', except:

0345. Call Morning Watch.
0355. Morning Watchmen to muster.
0700. Sea-boat's Crew of Forenoon Watch to clean into rig of the day.
0755. Sea-boat's Crews of Morning and Forenoon Watch to muster and relieve.

74. FOUL WEATHER ROUTINE

'A'—Harbour (Weekdays)

0505. Call Duty Boys' Instructors and Boy Cooks.
0535. Call all men under punishment.
0545. Call all Boys, Duty Petty Officers, Bugler and Emergency Party.
0550. Men under punishment to muster.
0600. Call the hands. Call away all Duty Boats' Crews. Clean, oil and water their boats. Emergency Party fall in. Fall out hammock stowers. Remainder place Wash Deck Gear and turn on Hoses. Morning Watch boys fall in.
0615. Up Guard and Steerage hammocks. Steerage Hammock Boys fall in.
0635. Uncover guns (if fine). Cooks.
0645. Hands to breakfast. Pipe rig of the day.
0720. 'G.'
0725. Out Pipes.
0730. Hands fall in. Stand fast Chief and Petty Officers' Messmen. Fall out Head and Scullery parties. Remainder scrub and wash the Upper deck.
0800. Dry down the Upper deck.
0815. Commander's Requestmen and Defaulters. 'G.'
0820. Hands to Quarters Clean Guns.
0830. Commander attends Requestmen and Defaulters.
0840. 'G.' Return rags.
0845. Both Watches of Hands fall in. Clean Messdecks and Flats. Finish off Upper deck. Clean bright-work.
0910. 'G.' Buglers' call. Cooks fall in when there are no Divisions.
0915. Divisions and Prayers. Then: both Watches fall in.

Then as for 'Daily Harbour Routine.'

'B'—Sea (Weekdays)

As for 'A', except:

0515.   Morning Watchmen to muster. Sweep down the Upper deck. Place Wash Deck Gear. Scrub Boat deck.

0635.   Fall out Morning Watchmen. Sea-boat's Crew of the Morning Watch to muster.

0755.   Sea-boat's Crews of Morning and Forenoon Watch to muster and relieve.

0900.   Sea-boat's Crew of Morning Watch fall in.

75. AFFILIATED SHIPS

The following is a copy of the notes sent to small ships when affiliated:

Notes for Ships Affiliated

(1) *General.*—We are anxious to do everything that we can to help you, so please do not hesitate to state your needs.

(2) *Boats.*—If at any time you are in difficulty in finding a boat to perform some special duty, let us know, and we will supply one if available.

(3) *Shipwrights and Joiners.*—Our staff is normally full up with work, but the requirements of the affiliated ships are given equal importance with our own work. Let us know what is wanted and we will do it if and when we can.

(4) *Workshops.*—Small repairs, including welding, can be carried out in our workshops. Whenever possible, materials should be supplied.

(5) *Clothing, Postal Orders and Provisions.*—It is requested that requirements of clothing or postal orders may be sent over in writing; on receipt of these a signal will be made informing you of the convenient date and time to send over an officer with the money, to draw the items required.

In the case of those ships requiring to draw fresh provisions, a signal should be made by 0800 daily of requirements for the following day. We will deliver these alongside the ship.

(6) *Ice.*—Small quantities of ice can be supplied on demand (twenty-four hours' notice in hot weather).

(7) *Cinema.*—A weekly show is given to small ships. Our boats will collect spectators.

Admission is twopence. Boys one penny. The Cinema is run on a contributory basis, the Canteen Fund paying about half of the cost of installation and the films.

(8) *Recreation.*—Any recreational facilities we possess are available for you on request. If any of your bayonetters, fencers, boxers or other warriors would like to train with ours at any time, they will be very welcome.

(9) *Long Baths (Officers).*—Long baths are available for you.

(10) *Canteen Managers and Messmen.*—If ours can be of any service to yours they are always ready to help.

(11) *Form S.549.*—When work is carried out for affiliated ships, involving expenditure of materials, the quantity so expended will normally be shown on a transfer note form S.549, and transferred to the store charge of the ship concerned. The necessary action to account for the expenditure can then be taken by the ship for which the work is done.

This procedure will not be necessary for minor jobs.

(12) *Signals.*—It is particularly requested that all signals in connection with any matter arising out of your affiliation to us may be addressed to the ship and not sent as private signals.

This ensures the correct distribution of the signal to all those concerned on board.